Christian Maturity

Christian Maturity

JAMES PHILIP

Minister of Holyrood Abbey
Church of Scotland, Edinburgh

INTER-VARSITY PRESS

Inter-Varsity Fellowship
39 Bedford Square, London WC1B 3EY

First edition March 1964
Reprinted 1964, 1966
Second edition (revised and reset) March 1973
ISBN 0 85110 366 9

This book is based on a series of addresses given at the IVF Swanwick Conference of Student Leaders held in September 1962.

Printed in Great Britain by
Hunt Barnard Printing Ltd., Aylesbury, Bucks.

Contents

Introduction

In all the wealth of teaching given in the Pauline Epistles on the nature of sanctification and the power of the indwelling Christ, probably no passage expresses so much truth in such brief compass as the remarkable statement in the Epistle to the Galatians: ' I have been crucified with Christ; it is no longer I who live, but Christ who lives in me; and the life I now live in the flesh I live by faith in the Son of God, who loved me and gave himself for me.'[1]

It would be difficult, indeed, to find any single verse containing more basic theology, for almost everything of final importance in Christian life and doctrine is to be found in it, either explicitly stated or implied — substitutionary atonement (' gave himself for me '), the mystery of the indwelling Christ (' Christ who lives in me '), our identification with Christ and our life in Him, the operation of the principle of faith, the glorious paradoxes of the Christian experience (crucified — living, ' no longer I who live, but Christ ').

This book is an attempt to present the apostle's teaching on this subject in both its objective and subjective aspects, and to unfold something of its significance

[1] Gal. 2:20.

in relation to the spiritual experience of the believer and his life of service for Christ. Its general outline, as will be seen from the chapter headings, covers such themes as the nature of the Christ who indwells the believer, the believer's spiritual union and identification with Him, the meaning of living by faith in the Son of God, and the expression of the new life in Christian behaviour and Christian character.

Two things may be said in this connection. Firstly, in following such a scheme the apostle's invariable practice is observed. One of the most striking and significant facts about the Pauline Epistles is his emphasis first of all on the great affirmations of the faith, and the basic facts of the gospel. It is only when he has unfolded the truth concerning Christ and His redemption that he proceeds to exhort his readers in terms of faith and consecration. The 'indicatives' of the gospel form the basis on which its 'imperatives' can be answered and fulfilled. Thus, in Romans, Paul devotes chapter after chapter to the systematic exposition of the gospel, and it is only in chapter 12 that he is ready to exhort his readers: 'I appeal to you therefore, brethren, by the mercies of God, to present your bodies as a living sacrifice, holy and acceptable to God, which is your spiritual worship.'[2]

It is the failing of evangelical ministry, very often, that it does not always follow this pattern in the preaching of the gospel, and this failure has led not only to the impoverishment of the corporate life of the church, but also to the charge of emotionalism being levelled against it — not without reason, since exhortation pressed without reference to any true foundation for it necessarily tends to have merely emotional effects.

Secondly, this order — indicatives followed by impera-

[2] Rom. 12:1.

tives — answers to the two basic problems and hindrances in spiritual life: lack of knowledge and understanding of the things of God on the one hand, and lack of will and intention to submit to them on the other. It may be said that there are two fundamental requirements for true growth and development in spiritual life: there are facts the believer needs to know, and grasp and understand — the truth needs to be expounded to him; and there is a moral submission of the heart and will to the truths he grasps; and it is the crowning challenge and summons of the gospel to bring him to that place of consecration and surrender. More will be said of this in a later chapter, but it is well to see at the outset what is the true nature of the gospel message, and what is the basis of its appeal to the heart, conscience and will of man.

CHAPTER ONE

The indwelling Christ

THE IMMEDIATE CONTEXT of the apostle's words in Galatians 2:20, a verse which has always been associated with the idea of sanctification, is in point of fact the fundamental issue of justification by faith apart from the works of the law. So far is he from being justified by the works of the law that he affirms: 'I through the law died to the law', and it is in this connection that he adds 'that I might live to God'. This he further expounds and explains in the following verse, 'I have been crucified with Christ. . . .' Thus, Galatians 2:20 stands as a necessary corollary of the idea of justification by faith, and it clearly indicates that for Paul justification and sanctification, although distinct from one another, can never be separated. This should be noted now, in relation to what will be said in a later chapter, in the fuller discussion of the meaning and implications of our union with Christ in His death and resurrection.

Paul's emphasis on the doctrine of justification at this juncture is significant and provides the true point of departure for any discussion on the Christ who indwells the believer and makes possible the life of faith. For it is here, first of all, in the understanding of the atonement Christ makes for men, that it becomes clear who He must be, and who He has to be, in order that atonement might be real.

The need for atonement

In a penetrating study, under the title *The Idea of Substitution in the Doctrine of the Atonement*,[1] F. W. Camfield writes: 'Man cannot atone. He cannot repair the past. Yet atonement, if it is to take place, must take place in man's life, and from man's side. How otherwise can it be atonement? . . . A deed issuing in a direct and unbroken line from the pure Godhead would not be atonement. Such a deed would inevitably be "over man's head". In order to be real atonement, it must issue forth from man's life.'

This underlines the dilemma — if it may without irreverence be so called — that faced God in the problem of man's redemption. Atonement — and therefore redemption — was not something God could accomplish by Himself by speaking a word of power, or even by an intervention in human history, as God. Man, as a moral being, is responsible for his sin, and therefore making amends for it is, from the ethical standpoint, essentially his responsibility also. But this is precisely what man cannot do, because in his sin he sins against the infinite God, and this gives it the character of the infinite in its extent and consequences. It is of the very essence of sin that it immediately passes out of man's control when once it is committed. He is no longer in a position either to cease from sin or to repair the past. Being infinite in its repercussions, it can be dealt with fully only by an infinite God.

[1] *Scottish Journal of Theology*, Vol. 1, No. 3, Dec. 1948.

The paradox of grace

This agonizing paradox, in which atonement must come necessarily from man's side, and is possible only from God's — with neither man as man, nor God as God able to provide it — is resolved once for all in the Person of Jesus Christ. As Camfield adds, 'The background of the atoning deed is not the Godhead *per se*, but the God-manhood of Christ.' The classical expression of this in the Creeds — 'Perfect God, and perfect Man' — gives us the key to the mystery, and J. H. Newman's great hymn sums up the thought admirably in the words:

> 'O generous love! that He who smote
> In Man for man, the foe,
> The double agony in Man,
> For man, should undergo.'

The God-man, Christ Jesus, uniting two natures, divine and human, in one Person makes complete atonement for sin. As a man, in man's life and from man's side, He makes atonement real; as God, in the infinite mystery of His Person, He makes it infinitely effectual. It is Jesus Christ the God-man who comes to live in our hearts by His Spirit. And this profound mystery must be thought into any real understanding of the doctrine and experience of the indwelling Christ.

The mystery of the incarnation

Something of the significance of this idea may be seen in the Prologue to the Fourth Gospel,[2] which expresses the profound mystery of the incarnation in language of

[2] Jn. 1:1-14.

sublime beauty and power. The force of John's contrast lies in the close juxtaposition of the words, 'All things were made through him' and 'The Word became flesh and dwelt among us'. It is the all-creating Word, Jesus Christ, who comes to dwell among men, the full implication of this amazing condescension being unfolded in the upper room discourse when, in His teaching about the Holy Spirit, Christ says of Him, 'He dwells with you, and will be in you.'[3]

An even more impressive statement, however, is made by the apostle Paul in the Epistle to the Colossians. It is here that the fullest answer is given to the question: 'Who is this Christ who dwells within us?' In the first chapter of the Epistle, in a passage full of sustained theological and spiritual insight, the apostle gives an exposition of the Person and work of Christ, with a particular purpose in view, which becomes plain in its concluding verses.

As to the Person of Christ, it is deity that Paul reveals, in a grandeur of description not surpassed even by John in his Prologue. Christ is the image of the invisible God,[4] the Creator of the ends of the earth;[5] He is before all things, and in Him all things hold together,[6] and life as we know it in the universe is held in being by His word and will; all fullness was pleased to dwell in Him;[7] the original 'Let there be light' was His word; the power that called the universe into being was His word; its glory and magnificence, its beauty and loveliness were all His work of creation, for He is God. It would be difficult to find a more sublime exposition of the greatness and majesty of Christ anywhere in literature.

[3] Jn. 14:17.
[4] Col. 1:15.
[5] Col. 1:16.
[6] Col. 1:17.
[7] Col. 1:19.

Cosmic reconciliation

Having spoken in such absolute terms about the Person of Christ, the apostle then describes the work He came to accomplish. Reconciliation — significantly, as will be seen later — is the word he uses. He speaks, however, not only of the reconciliation of man to God, but first of all of the reconciliation of 'all things, whether on earth, or in heaven',[8] and then, as part of this, man's reconciliation. What Paul is referring to is the removal of the disorder wrought in the entire created universe by sin, a removal effected by the power of Christ's death.

> 'His the nails, the spear, the spitting,
> Reed and vinegar and gall;
> From his patient body pierced
> Blood and water streaming fall;
> Earth and sea and stars and mankind
> By that stream are cleansed all.'

This is a note Paul strikes elsewhere in his writings,[9] where he speaks of the creation waiting with eager longing for the revealing of the sons of God, that it might itself be delivered from its bondage to decay and share in the glorious liberty of the children of God. 'The whole creation', he adds, 'has been groaning in travail together until now.' In the deepest, truest sense, it is a *cosmic* Christ that Paul presents in his Epistles, and certainly in Colossians.

Now — and this is the point of the tremendous climactic piece of writing — it is such a Christ who dwells in the believer as the hope of glory,[1] the Christ who is the Creator of all things and the Reconciler of all creation, living in him, exercising His creative power and His

[8] Col. 1:20. [9] Rom. 8:19-22. [1] Col. 1:27.

reconciling ministry. It would be difficult to overestimate the possibilities for spiritual life inherent in a true appreciation of this glorious conception. It means that He who created the rugged grandeur of the everlasting hills may indwell a human heart to impart a similar moral grandeur and ruggedness. He who brought into being the beauty and fragrance of the rose may come to lives stained and marred by sin and transform them with a similar moral and spiritual grace. He who holds the universe in being by the word of His power may make men's hearts His dwelling-place; and can it be that He will not be able to keep those hearts in order? He who holds all worlds in His hand undertakes to hold the reins of men's lives. All fullness dwells in Him, and He dwells in the believer!

The all-glorious Christ

There comes to mind the vision given to John on Patmos of Christ in majesty.[2] In this tremendous description — head and hair white as white wool, white as snow, eyes like a flame of fire, feet like burnished bronze, voice like the sound of many waters, face like the sun shining in full strength — the impression that is created, and surely it is meant to be so, is one of greatness and overwhelming power. It is the magnitude of the conception that staggers the thought and the imagination. It is this Christ, this figure of unique grandeur and majesty, who is the power whose indwelling transforms and transfigures the life of the believer. There is little doubt that when the New Testament speaks of the

[2] Rev. 1:13-18.

reality of the indwelling Christ, it thinks of Him pre-eminently in this way.

It is true that the humanity of Christ is essentially relevant in a true understanding of the nature and significance of His indwelling — and this will be a matter for serious consideration presently — but this relevance is subject to the condition of faith in the exalted, all-glorious Christ, who has been given a name that is above every name. This, as Dr James Denney repeatedly insisted, is the heart and essence of New Testament theology. 'The subject', says Denney, 'of the apostle's Gospel was not Jesus the carpenter of Nazareth, but Christ the Lord of glory; men, as he understood the matter, were saved, not by dwelling on the wonderful words and deeds of One who had lived some time ago, and reviving these in their imagination, but by receiving the almighty, emancipating, quickening Spirit of One Who lived and reigned for evermore.'[3] Nothing less than this understanding of the divine indwelling is sufficient to account for the wonderful, transforming experience known by the early church in its personal and corporate life. The dull lifelessness of much Christian experience at the present time is a measure of the poverty-stricken nature of the church's conception of Christ. Our God, to use J. B. Phillips' pregnant phrase, is too small.

The man Christ Jesus

The thought of the deity of Christ, however, in relation to the divine indwelling does not exhaust the possibilities of spiritual enrichment. He is God, but He is

[3] Denney, *2 Corinthians*, p. 140.

also man, the second, or last, Adam, and in the incarnation He has come, as John puts it in his Prologue, to dwell or 'tabernacle' with men. He is Emmanuel, God with us. The ultimate implication of the incarnation is expressed in the last words of Matthew's Gospel: 'Lo, I am with you always, to the close of the age.' The incarnation really means that God in Christ has united Himself to humanity for ever. This is, in point of fact, the significance of the doctrine of the ascension, for it teaches the eternal manhood of the exalted and glorified Christ. His identification with man must not be thought of as a temporary expedient, but as something permanent, and for ever. It is necessary therefore to think also of the humanity of the ascended Lord in relation to His indwelling the hearts of His people. This will be seen to have practical implications for the life of the believer, and will be dealt with fully in a later section.

Christ's identification with man was complete. The words of Ezekiel, describing his association with the captives at Tel-abib — 'I sat where they sat'[4] — may be fitly used to describe our Lord's union with mankind in its sin and need. This in fact is the story of the incarnation, when He entered into man's life and took his flesh and nature. He was born into our life, born for us. And He lived as man, for us, living our life, sharing its toils and cares and burdens. He was baptized for us, and in that act He took His stand with men in their sin, 'repenting' for us, as it were, vicariously. In like manner, He was tempted for us — tempted in every respect just as we are, yet without sinning — identifying Himself with this incontrovertible reality in human life and experience.

[4] Ezk. 3:15, AV.

The indictment

This total identification can be seen perhaps more graphically in His trial than at any other point. For His death had to be preceded by the trial precisely for the reason that, in associating Himself with man in his sin, it was man's judicial condemnation that He bore. There was a twofold count brought against Christ; He was charged with both blasphemy and treason, blasphemy being the ecclesiastical charge, and treason the political. These in fact constitute man's indictment at the bar of divine justice. The element of blasphemy in human sin is too stark and obvious to be ignored. When Satan tempted Adam and Eve in the garden, his incitement was: 'You will be like God', and this grimly lucid picture from the book of Genesis is meant to remind us that man in his sin trespasses upon the divine prerogatives and makes himself, to use the late William Temple's phrase, 'the centre of the world'.

This propensity in man to make himself a god can only be described as blasphemy. It was precisely to avoid this terrible pitfall that restriction was placed on Adam in the garden. The prohibition, 'Of the tree of the knowledge of good and evil you shall not eat', was made to remind him of his creatureliness. In yielding, therefore, to the temptation Adam not only committed blasphemy, but was also guilty of treason, in that he deliberately rebelled against the known will and command of God.

It was because of this that Christ remained silent during the trial, saying nothing that might have vindicated His position, when He could, as He had said, have called upon twelve legions of angels to help Him. He did not *wish* to be delivered, because He chose freely to take man's place and bear man's condemnation, with all that this involved. So closely did He identify Himself with mankind. And the cross is simply the consummation of this constant principle. The statement, ' He took our place ', is true not only of the death that He died, but also of every stage in His experience, and continues beyond it. He rose for us,[5] and ascended for us, entering into heaven for us, as the Epistle to the Hebrews puts it.[6] And when His finished work was crowned by the coming of the Spirit at Pentecost, *that* Counsellor came simply to fulfil and make permanent and lasting the pattern that had been unfolded during His earthly life. For He came as *another* Counsellor, an *alter Christus*, as the early Fathers used to say, that He might be with us for ever. For, as Christ said, ' He dwells with you, and will be in you.'[7]

The mighty advocate

It is at this point that the thought of the high priesthood of Christ naturally comes to mind. For He is our advocate with the Father, and an advocate is one who is identified with the person whose cause he has espoused and undertaken to plead. Thus we read in the Epistle to the Hebrews: ' It is plain that for this purpose he did not become an angel; he became a *man*, in actual fact a descendant of Abraham. It was imperative that he should be made like his brothers in nature, if he were to become a High Priest both compassionate and faithful in the things of God, and at the same time able to make atonement for the sins of the people ';[8] and again, ' We have no superhuman High Priest to whom our weak-

[5] Rom. 4:25. [6] Heb. 9:24. [7] Jn. 14:16, 17.
[8] Heb. 2:16, 17, J. B. Phillips' translation.

nesses are unintelligible — he himself has shared fully in all our experience of temptation, except that he never sinned.'[9] Thus completely could He claim (to use Ezekiel's words again) to have ' sat where they sat '; thus closely did He associate Himself with man. In the mystery of His God-manhood, deity and manhood are both alike revealed — and indeed communicated to men — in His identification with them.

Christ — able and willing

Two contrasting incidents in our Lord's healing ministry serve to illuminate this whole theme. In the story of the demon-possessed boy at the foot of the Mount of Transfiguration, the father appealed to Christ in the words, ' If you can do anything, have pity on us and help us.'[1] It was, in effect, an appeal to Christ's humanity that he made, to His compassion and fellow-feeling for him in his need. In the way he expressed his plea, however, he expressed doubt as to His power to do so. In contrast to this, in the story of the cleansing of the leper, the latter is recorded to have cried, ' If you will, you can make me clean.'[2] Here the attitude is quite different. There was no doubt in the leper's mind as to whether Christ could cleanse him: he was obviously convinced that He could. What did concern him was whether He would. In other words, while there was a definite conviction in his heart about Christ's power — doubtless born in him through hearing Christ preach on the mount — there was a doubt about His willingness to cleanse.

The reactions of these two men are significant; the

[9] Heb. 4:15, J. B. Phillips' translation.
[1] Mk. 9:22. [2] Mt. 8:2.

one had, in effect, doubts as to the Godhead of Christ, the other doubts as to His humanity. And the instances stand in the sacred record that men might be convinced of both His ability and His willingness to help them. In the mystery of His God-manhood, power and compassion unite to heal man's immemorial wound and assuage the inconsolable ache in his heart.

Such is the Christ who comes to indwell the hearts of men by faith — *this* cosmic Figure, Author of all worlds, *this* Man of sorrows, whose human heart goes out to the weakness and agony of man, who is moved with compassion in face of human woe, and says ' I will ' — *this* Christ ' lives in me '.

CHAPTER TWO

Union with Christ

HAVING DEALT WITH Christ's identification with man in His coming, as the God-man, to be the Saviour of the world, it is now necessary to turn to the complementary truth: union and identification with Him in His death and resurrection as the heart of the Christian experience of sanctification. This central idea in Pauline theology is expressed also in the words of the apostle already referred to: 'I am crucified with Christ: nevertheless I live.'[1]

This is a truth not always understood or grasped as it ought to be. People either do not know it at all, or they know it in a confused and even distorted fashion. It will be necessary, therefore, to study it in some detail.

What is a Christian?

A convenient point of departure may be found in a consideration of the question: 'What exactly happens to a man when he becomes a believer in the New Testament sense?' The fullest possible answer is given in Paul's exposition of the gospel in his Epistle to the Romans. Those who are familiar with the structure of

[1] Gal. 2:20, AV.

that brilliant piece of writing will know that in its first three chapters the apostle is concerned to bring home a verdict upon man as sinner, and with inexorable logic he presses his conclusions upon his readers, indicating that man in his sin is involved in a threefold predicament: he is *under wrath*:[2] his ungodliness and unrighteousness incur the divine anger. He is *under condemnation*:[3] his sin has violated the divine law and made him accountable to its penalty. He is *under sin*:[4] here sin is conceived of as a power that holds him in bondage.

Having completed his 'case' and established his verdict, the apostle proceeds to unfold and proclaim the riches of the good news in Christ, God's mighty intervention in the human situation to put man right with Himself, by justifying them that believe in Jesus:

> 'But now the righteousness of God has been manifested apart from law . . . the righteousness of God through faith in Jesus Christ for all who believe. For there is no distinction; since all have sinned and fall short of the glory of God, they are justified by his grace as a gift, through the redemption which is in Christ Jesus, whom God put forward as a propitiation by his blood, to be received by faith.'[5]

In this gloriously rich theological statement, Paul uses three words which answer the threefold count he has brought against man in his sin. In the first place, his being under wrath is met by the idea of *propitiation*. This fundamentally biblical concept indicates that in the death of Christ the divine anger against man is turned

[2] Rom. 1:18. [3] Rom. 3:19. [4] Rom. 3:9.
[5] Rom. 3:21-25; it is interesting that the latest edition of the RSV has restored the word 'propitiation' in this passage.

away, and that the controversy God has with the sinner is now at an end. Secondly, man's condemnation is met by the idea of *justification*. The guilt of his sin has been laid upon Christ, who stands in the place of condemnation for him, and Christ's righteousness is 'imputed' or made over to him, thus making him acceptable to God. Thirdly, his bondage to sin is met by the idea of *redemption*.

Many Christians are familiar and conversant with the doctrine implied in the words *propitiation* and *justification*. They know that when a man believes in Christ his sins are forgiven; that the divine anger is turned away by the blood of Christ which speaks peace to the holy heart of God as well as to the sinful heart of man; that he is justified by faith and that there can be no more condemnation for his sin. This, in fact, is the substitutionary aspect of the atonement.

Man in bondage

But justification and propitiation alone do not exhaust the meaning Paul is expressing in this passage. For, as indicated above, sin is more than the grim reality that incurs divine wrath and brings guilt upon men. Sin is a power under which men are held, as by a despotic and merciless ruler. In a later passage in the Epistle Paul speaks of it as 'reigning in death', and the Greek phrase might very fairly be translated 'sin became king'.[6]

The meaning of redemption

It is this aspect of sin that is met in the idea expressed by the word *redemption*, the root meaning of which is 'to

[6] Rom. 5:21.

release, or set free, by the payment of a price'. It is a picture taken from the slave-market and, according to Dr Leon Morris in *The Apostolic Preaching of the Cross*,[7] there are three main ideas associated with its usage. One is the state of sin out of which men are bought by the blood of Christ. The gospel is the intervention of an outside power who pays the price to release us. Another is the price that is paid. The purchase price of our redemption is the blood of the Redeemer. The third idea is the resultant state; we are bought out of bondage into the glorious liberty of the children of God.

Basically, therefore, the idea of redemption includes the thought of new life. A new situation is created when redemption takes place. What happens to a man who becomes a believer is that, in believing, he is not only pardoned and accepted by God, but also set free and brought into a new relationship with Christ; and this means not only fellowship *with* Christ, but fellowship *in* Christ. This new life, which is the new birth, is by the Spirit of God.[8] As Paul says elsewhere, 'By one Spirit we were all baptized into one body.'[9]

To be born again is, therefore, to be born into Christ, into union with Him. This is basic to the very idea of salvation as Paul understands it, and it is this that he proceeds in subsequent chapters of Romans to unfold. Thus, the all-important sixth chapter of the Epistle is in fact nothing more or less than an explanation and an exposition of what he has said earlier on the subject of justification by faith, and no understanding of this greatest of Epistles is possible until this fact is grasped. The characteristic phraseology of the apostle in this connection — 'believe on the Lord Jesus Christ' — means, as the Greek indicates, 'believe *into* the Lord

[7] Tyndale Press, 1955. [8] Jn. 3:3-8. [9] 1 Cor. 12:13.

Jesus Christ' (*pisteuō eis*), and makes it clear that the act of faith 'incorporates' a man into Christ and into union with His death and resurrection.

The miracle of grace

This idea of 'incorporation' into Christ is important and its significance and implications require to be understood. In such a passage as Philippians 2:5 ff., the picture Paul has in mind in describing the gospel is that of a parabola — the downward movement of Christ from the glory of heaven to the cross of shame, followed by the upward movement to the right hand of the Father. It is when this 'movement' touches a human life and 'takes it up', so to speak, into itself, that the miracle of grace takes place. Men are thus 'incorporated' into Christ and into His finished work — into His 'movement' indeed, in the sense that they partake of its power and virtue. What must be understood is that at that point where Christ was made in the likeness of sinful flesh, He laid hold of sinful nature, on His way down, so to speak, into the murky depths, and took it *into* death with Him, and *through* death with Him, and *up out of* death with Him, into the glory of resurrection life.

It is when spiritual conversion is looked at in this light that it is seen to involve not only justification, as has already been pointed out, but also a being brought into union with Christ's death and resurrection. Thus, to have faith not only means to be justified, but also to be crucified with Christ and risen with Him. This is what the apostle means by the words, 'I am (Gk. "have been") crucified with Christ; nevertheless I live.'[1] A

[1] Gal. 2:20, AV.

moment's reflection will show how basic this idea is, not only to Paul's theology but to the whole teaching of the New Testament. In the Acts of the Apostles Paul describes his appeal to men in the preaching of the gospel as urging ' repentance to God and . . . faith in our Lord Jesus Christ '.[2] Repentance and faith are therefore correlatives and complementary to one another. To turn to Christ — which is what faith means — is to turn one's back upon sin, to repent of it, to die to it. It is this death, which is man's response to Christ's death and made possible by it, which is the vital element in a living faith, enabling him to say, as Paul did, ' I have been crucified with Christ.' The faith that justifies, in other words, is a faith that crucifies. And yet it is not to die, it is to live. We live — this is the miracle — but it is the life of Another in us, His life by the Spirit. This is the meaning of re-birth by the Spirit of God, by which a man becomes a Christian.

The basic theology underlying this ' death-life ' pattern must now be examined, and in this connection it is essential to grasp the significance of Paul's teaching in Romans 5:12-21, where, in a closely-knit paragraph which makes difficult reading, he unfolds certain basic principles which it is necessary to understand before the force of his subsequent statements in Romans 6, or their crucial significance, can possibly be grasped.

Adam and Christ

First of all, the thread of Paul's argument in this complicated passage must be distinguished, and that is best done by reading verses 12 and 18 together, omitting for the moment verses 13-17, which are a kind of parenthesis.

[2] Acts 20:21.

What the apostle is saying is: ' As by one man, Adam, sin entered into the world, bringing death in its train, and condemnation upon all mankind, even so the righteousness of One, Jesus Christ, brings life and justification.' If there were any doubts as to the validity of this interpretation, they are dispelled by the clear and unequivocal statement which Paul makes in the Corinthian Epistle: ' As in Adam all die, so also in Christ shall all be made alive.'[3]

That this is a by no means easy concept is proved by the controversy that raged over the proper translation of the last phrase in verse 12, ' because all men sinned '. Earlier commentators, following Augustine, rendered it, ' in whom (*i.e.* in Adam) all have sinned ', while the weight of modern opinion, following Sanday and Headlam in the *International Critical Commentary*, is in favour of ' inasmuch as all have sinned '. However, notwithstanding the impressive arguments in favour of the latter rendering, it should surely be clear from the whole context of the paragraph that Paul cannot mean that because all men have sinned they share Adam's fate. If he had meant that all men become subject to death because of the sins they have committed, the logical conclusion of his argument would be that they also enter into life because of the righteousness they achieve. And this is the exact opposite of what he does say here. There would also be no point in having said it. But on the contrary it is through the righteousness of One that men enter into life, and the apostle's argument at this point requires the other idea, namely that all men have sinned in Adam. It is in fact the only thing he could mean, in this context, however difficult an idea it may be to accept. Doubtless there is an element

[3] 1 Cor. 15:22.

of contradiction in it, but it is a contradiction borne out by man's own experience, for in his truest and deepest thoughts about sin he knows both that he is responsible for it, and also that, in some tragic way that may never fully be understood, it is something he cannot help and over which he does not have final control.

Mankind's solidarity in sin

The apostle proceeds in verses 13 and 14 to justify his teaching by pointing out that the reality of this solidarity in sin is quite unmistakable even in those who have not sinned, as Adam did, by direct disobedience of a command of God. Death, he says, held sway over mankind from Adam to Moses, before the coming of the law made sin technically ' an offence ' and therefore accountable as guilt. This is seen very graphically in the fact that infants sometimes die before they can possibly have committed actual transgression. They do not die because they have *committed* sin, but because, in the far deeper sense, they have sinned in Adam, that is to say, they partake of fallen human nature and belong, in Adam, to a humanity under the curse and shadow of death. Death reigns as a cruel tyrant over the whole of humanity and, as one commentator puts it, does not ask man whether he will serve him, but rules autocratically over him.

The apostle is therefore comparing and contrasting two different orders of existence, described in the phrases ' in Adam ' and ' in Christ '. In the earlier chapters of Romans he describes man's predicament ' in Adam ', in the old order of existence, and here man is under condemnation and in the bondage of sin. But ' in Christ ' he is brought into a new order of existence; he is delivered out of the kingdom of darkness and transferred into the kingdom of God's dear Son.[4]

Underlying this contrast of ' orders ' is a thought that simply must be grasped before any real understanding of Paul's teaching is possible, namely that humanity is regarded as a single body under a single head. Adam is, of course, a historical figure to Paul, but in the Scripture record and in the apostle's theology he stands not merely as a private individual, and it is not in this capacity that he speaks of him. He is a representative figure, a public person, the head of the race, and what he did involved the whole race of mankind which he represented. And when condemnation and death passed upon Adam they came upon him as the head of the race, and thus they ' spread to all men '.

Christ's victory and ours

Christ, on the other hand, is the last Adam, the head of the new order, also a representative Figure, and what He did (on the cross) involves all who are ' in him '. According to Paul, all men are ' in ' the one or the other.

This idea of representative figures is quite common in daily life and in Scripture alike. A member of Parliament, for example, is a representative figure, and government by representation of the people is a cardinal element in the British way of life. An MP does not sit in the House of Commons as a private person, but in a representative capacity. When he votes, his constituents vote ' in ' him. Similarly, at gatherings such as the Trades Union Congress, when the result of a ballot vote is reckoned in terms of hundreds of thousands of

[4] Col. 1:13.

votes, it does not mean that hundreds of thousands of Trade Union members were present in person, but only that they were represented by duly appointed delegates, each of whom carried a block, or representative, vote. Individual members vote 'in' them and 'in' their vote.

The Old Testament story of David and Goliath[5] illustrates the idea perfectly. It was agreed by both Israelites and Philistines that a victory for Goliath would 'count as' a victory for the whole Philistine army, and a victory for David likewise for all Israel. In other words, they fought not as private warriors, but as the representatives of their respective armies. Significantly, when the Philistines saw their champion was dead, they fled, recognizing in his defeat their own.

So it is with Adam and Christ. Adam 'lost' the battle in the Garden of Eden and his side 'lost' in him. Christ won the battle on the cross and all His side 'gain' the victory in Him. This is Paul's teaching here, and it is basic to all he says about our union with Christ.

Through faith, a man is grafted into Christ, that is to say, he is translated from the old order of humanity, in Adam, into the new, in Christ. This change takes place at the moment of justification. The same faith that appropriates justification in the substitutionary death of Christ also brings him into Christ, into a union with Him in His death and resurrection. Justification and union with Christ are both involved in the same act of faith, so much so that it can truly be said that the faith that justifies is a faith which crucifies. The apostle's words: 'I have been crucified with Christ',[6] refer to something that takes place at conversion. It is not something to be sought after as an advanced stage of

[5] 1 Sa. 17:9, 51. [6] Gal. 2:20.

Christian experience; it is an accomplished fact from the outset, when a man puts his trust in Christ.

Sin and the believer

The sixth chapter of Romans is the exposition of this truth, and it might almost have been written expressly for the benefit of those who had not appreciated the force of what the apostle has written in the immediately preceding passage.[7] This is the whole point of the series of questions he poses in this central and fundamental section of the Epistle.

The question that is put to him, 'Are we to continue in sin, that grace may abound?'[8] arises from the statement made at the end of the previous chapter, 'where sin increased, grace abounded all the more'.[9] The apostle is shocked into a swift retort by such a question. It is as if he were saying, 'The man who says such a thing simply shows he has failed to understand what I have been teaching up to this point. How could a man continue in sin if he has died to it? Do you not understand what it was that happened to you when you professed Christ? Do you not realize that if you have trusted in Christ for salvation at all, this is the truth about you, that you have died to sin? If you are a believer, then this is where God has placed you, these are the facts about your position now — you are dead, crucified, buried, with Christ. The old man — the man you once were — has been crucified with Christ, that the sinful self might be destroyed, that you might no longer be enslaved to sin.'

[7] Rom. 5:12-21. [8] Rom. 6:1. [9] Rom. 5:20.

Dead to sin — alive to God

Obviously, then, the apostle is assuming, or had assumed, that his readers (or questioners) realized that to believe in Christ[1] and to have died to sin are one and the same thing. He proceeds, consequently, to underline this point in the following verses. Six times he states in different terms the central truth that we died to sin in the death of Christ. We are 'baptized into his death';[2] we are 'buried with him';[3] we are 'united with him in a death like his';[4] we are 'crucified with him',[5] we 'have died',[6] and 'have died with Christ'.[7] It should be noted particularly that Paul is here dealing with objective facts, with what Christ has done for us, and not with things we do or experience. His statements are in the indicative, not the imperative, mood.

To grasp this is to be saved from a fundamental misunderstanding of Paul's teaching. It is sometimes thought that the apostle is here teaching: 'You must die to sin', but it cannot be too strongly emphasized that this is not the case. That would be an exhortation, an imperative. What he *is* teaching is — and this is the grand, liberating message — 'You *have died* to sin in the death of Christ.' It is a statement of fact. It is not something man does, but something God has done, in the death of His Son. And it is because it is a statement of fact first that it can become a truth in experience.

This, then, is what it means to be a Christian, what it means to be converted. A man cannot be forgiven without at the same time being this! Being crucified with Christ is what 'being a Christian' means. This is where faith has placed us, where God has placed us, and

[1] Rom. 3:26; 4:24; 5:1. [2] Rom. 6:3. [3] Rom. 6:4.
[4] Rom. 6:5. [5] Rom. 6:6. [6] Rom. 6:7. [7] Rom. 6:8.

we must allow God to tell us where we now are. Such is our position, and this is what we are summoned to believe in the message of the gospel. 'What the law could never do, because our lower nature robbed it of all potency, God has done: by sending his own Son in a form like that of our own sinful nature, and as a sacrifice for sin, he has passed judgement against sin within that very nature. . . .'[8] That is to say, He has passed a sentence of condemnation on it, sent it to the death cell, so to speak, putting it under lock and key, to await final execution.

This is the happy truth about a man who has put his trust in Christ and become a believer, and he is to 'reckon' upon it.[9] These are the facts, and they must be recognized as facts and acted upon.

Fact, faith and experience

It may be noted at this point that the passage under consideration has a threefold emphasis. In verses 1-10 of Romans 6 the apostle is unfolding the facts of the situation; in verses 11-13, it is the activity of faith that he has in mind, that is, man's response to the facts; while in verse 14 he speaks of the experience of the believer. The point he is making is surely plain: it is that, when the facts of the gospel are laid hold of by a living faith, a certain result will always follow, in which the believer will be liberated from the bondage and dominion of sin. This order is basic to all true Christian thinking. The quality of spiritual experience always depends on faith — 'according to your faith be it done to you',[1] said Christ. But, in turn, the quality of faith depends upon a true understanding and grasp of the

[8] Rom. 8:3, NEB. [9] Rom. 6:11, AV. [1] Mt. 9:29.

facts which are the foundation of faith. That is, why Paul lays such an emphasis on faith's recognition of the facts of the gospel in verse 11, for recognition will lead to action. Indeed, faith in this sense *is* action, the action of refusing to let sin reign in our mortal bodies. And everything depends on this.

The doctrine becomes operative as a living reality in experience only when it is believed, only when the truths it unfolds are accepted, only when the facts are recognized to be facts and acted upon — in precisely the same way as the message that Christ died for our sins becomes operative only when we reckon upon it, and believe and accept the truth to be truth for us personally.

The mighty work of our crucifixion with Christ[2] took place fundamentally, and once for all, on the cross centuries ago, in the reign of Pontius Pilate; it becomes actual in our experience the moment we trust in Christ — just as our pardon was won fundamentally and once for all long ago, but becomes actual in experience when we believe the gospel. Nor should this — the destruction of ' the old self ', or nature — be any more difficult to understand and believe than the fact that the guilt of our sin was dealt with in the cross. Indeed, ' believing that our guilt was done away in the cross ' is meant to have included within that act of faith the parallel and complementary truth that ' our old self was crucified with him ' also. In neither case is the connection between our sin — whether considered as guilt or bondage — and His death a logical one, but rather spiritual and eternal. In both, however, the connection is the same, and when the facts are reckoned upon, the promised experience will always result.

[2] Rom. 6:6.

Challenge to faith

This then is the challenge to faith. We must dare to believe God when He tells us the facts about ourselves in His Word, and live in the light of His view of us, not our own. However, the trouble is that we do not know, and do not seem to be able to believe the truth about ourselves — hence Paul's oft-repeated question in Romans 6, 'Do you not know . . . ?' This is the crux of the whole matter.

A simple illustration will help to make this clear. A bride may not, in the first moments of her marriage, sufficiently realize her new status to recognize that it is she who is being addressed when the officiating clergyman calls her by her married name. In such a situation it would be true to say that for the moment she did not know who she was. In the spiritual life this is precisely the trouble. We do not know who we are, or what we are, in Christ. If we did, we would live very differently from the way we do. We would say to ourselves: 'Up to now I have not known my true identity. I have thought my sin inevitable. Now, in the light of what God says has happened to me in the death of His Son, I will be the new man He has made me. I will no longer act as though I were still the man I used to be. I will be the man God says I am. I will say to sin, "I refuse to be dominated any longer by you. I am the Lord's freeman, and I am ready for anything through the strength of the One who lives within me".'

Only thus is it possible to fulfil the ethical obligations of the gospel.

Ignorance the enemy

The establishment of his true identity — this is the believer's greatest need. As long as there remains ignorance or misunderstanding of his true riches and wealth in Christ, so long will his spiritual life remain impoverished and his service in the gospel stunted and ineffective, a shadow of what it might have been. The prevalence of so much fruitless work in the church in our generation, in spite of often lavish expenditure of time and talents and resources, makes it all the more urgently imperative to re-examine foundations and re-discover the true inspiration and dynamic of the life that tells for God.

CHAPTER THREE

Saved in hope

THE DIFFICULTY EXPERIENCED by many in grasping the truth and implications of the believer's union with Christ in His death and resurrection suggests that there are problems in interpretation that require elucidation. These problems arise in the main from the disparity between the teaching of the apostle and the conscious experience of the believer in the matter of sanctification. This whole area needs to be explored more fully and in more detail than has hitherto been possible in the formal exposition of the doctrine, and to it we now turn.

The questions that arise are these: 1. In what sense can it be said that we are now free from sin? 2. Is the apostle teaching that the old nature is abolished and no longer in existence? 3. How can we believe that 'the old self' has been 'crucified with Christ' and 'the sinful body destroyed' when we are conscious day by day, in our heartsore experience, of what Paul calls 'our sinful passions . . . in our members'? 4. And what are we to say of Romans 7 with its agonizing conflict and cry of despair at the end? Does not this call in question any confident assertion that the destruction of the old nature is an accomplished fact?

Defining terms

The answer to these very real questions lies in the proper understanding of Pauline terminology. Our difficulties arise because we tend to give to the word 'sin' a meaning which falls short of the apostle's. In his writings, and in the New Testament generally, sin is spoken of, not so much in terms of isolated moral misdeeds, as of an authority under which we live. The word he uses in Romans 5 is *basileuō* which means 'to reign as a king'. To be set free from sin means, therefore, to be delivered from this authority that lords it over mankind. There is no thought in Paul's mind here of becoming sinless. It is safe to say that this idea is foreign to the whole thinking of the New Testament, and it would not have occurred to any of its writers to speak in such terms, for the very reason that they think of sin in terms not so much of individual acts as of a terrible oppressive power. When the apostle spoke of freedom from sin, it was in the sense that Christ has now become the new Authority in the life of the believer, in place of the former despotic reign of sin. (That sinlessness cannot be in Paul's mind is also borne out by the fact that he exhorts his readers not to let sin reign in their mortal bodies, an exhortation that would have been meaningless and unnecessary if freedom from sin had meant sinlessness. He certainly recognized that sin was still a possibility for the one who has been set free from sin!)

The two worlds

There is, in fact, a paradox in Paul's teaching in Romans 6, in which two seemingly contrasting truths are held together in tension. On the one hand, the destruction of ' the sinful body ' is spoken of as an accomplished fact; on the other hand, the believer is urged to resist sin, and not allow it to reign over him, as if the attainment of victory were something he himself had to accomplish. The contradiction is only apparent, for the believer lives in two worlds; he is ' in Christ ', but he is also, at the same time, ' in the flesh ', and the new life that is his through grace has to be lived out, and finds its expression in the sphere of the old life. Therefore, side by side with the truth that we are ' free from sin ' and ' dead to sin ' there is also the other truth that we must ' do battle with sin ', otherwise it will regain control of that which it has lost and bring us again into bondage. As Nygren points out,[1] a prisoner of war is powerless to act against the enemy while in captivity; only when he is liberated from the prison camp can he fight against him on the victory side, and from the standpoint of liberty.

This can be put another way. It has already been suggested that when Paul speaks of God having ' condemned sin in the flesh ' he means not merely that He expressed disapproval of sin, but that He passed a sentence of death upon the old nature, placing it, so to speak, under lock and key. This is a useful, if picturesque, metaphor, for it underlines the fact that condemned criminals have been known to escape from prison! The believer must see to it that ' he ' — the ' old self ', as Paul puts it — is kept in his proper place in captivity. Hence Paul can say: ' Let not sin therefore reign in your mortal bodies.'[2]

[1] I am indebted to A. Nygren's *Commentary on Romans* (S.C.M., 1962) for the elucidation of this whole section of the apostle's argument.

[2] Rom. 6:12.

Freedom in Christ

In the light of these considerations it should now be possible to understand more fully what Paul means when he says that 'our old self was crucified with him, so that the sinful body might be destroyed'.[3] The word 'destroyed' cannot, it is clear, mean 'abolished' in the sense of being put out of existence. Weymouth translates the word as 'deprived of its power' and this is a useful pointer in assessing Paul's meaning. The same word (*katargeō*) is used in the Epistle to the Hebrews[4] of the destruction of the devil. It does not mean that the devil is put out of existence — we know only too well that he is still to be reckoned with! — but we believe that, in the death of Christ, his power was once for all broken, and that he no longer holds the initiative in the life of the believer.

This is a good parallel, and the 'destruction' of 'the old self' must be thought of in just the same way. The New English Bible translates 'our old self' as 'the man we once were' and this also is helpful, for it means that Paul is saying: 'Sin is a cruel bondage, and by nature, habit, choice, men are slaves to its power. That is what we once were — in bondage to sin. But now in Christ we are no longer that. We have been set free.'

A simple illustration may serve to throw further light on yet another aspect of this question. The writer once heard a teacher of theology describe a visit he had paid to Canada. It was winter time and the St Lawrence river was completely frozen over. But when spring came, people began eagerly to await the great thaw. Presently the ice cracked and the freeze-up was over. But for some time afterwards ice-floes could be

[3] Rom. 6:6. [4] Heb. 2:14.

seen coming down the river. The freeze-up had been broken in principle, but there was still ice to be seen. The power that had gripped the river was no longer in control, although there were still evidences of its former dominion to be seen. So it is with the bondage and authority of sin, and this illustrates how it is possible for a believer, who has truly been set free from its tyranny, still to have evidences of sin in his life.

The need for appropriation

This still leaves unanswered, however, the dilemma arising from the believer's consciousness of the wide disparity between the teaching of the apostle and his own heartsore experience. The explanation nevertheless is a simple one: what Paul teaches is a truth of *fact* before it becomes a truth of *experience*, and must be grasped as such, and believed, before its powers can be known. It is in fact true in the same sense as it is true that in the cross the guilt of our sin is done away. The message of Christ crucified is that the sin of the whole world has been cancelled; but guilt is a reality, notwithstanding, to every unconverted soul. The fundamental, once-for-all atonement must be appropriated personally before forgiveness and peace can be a reality in experience. Not only so; in the life of a believer it is by no means unknown for very real feelings of guilt to cause distress and disturbance, sometimes to such an extent that all sense of the peace of God is lost.

Anyone who is familiar with the writings of John Bunyan will know how true this is. But why should it be? It is because there is a devil who accuses the brethren[5] and stirs up in them something that has

[5] Rev. 12:10.

already been put to rest by God. May he not likewise stir up 'the old self' that has been crucified, to cause the believer endless trouble, and call in question the whole fabric of the divine teaching? Must we not at times dare to believe God and allow Him to tell us where He has placed us in the death of His Son, and rest upon this in the very teeth of the devil's lies and all the evidence of our own hearts?

Christ or law?

It is here, perhaps, that a discussion of the meaning of the much-disputed passage in Romans 7 should take place. This memorable utterance emerges from Paul's teaching about the relation of the gospel to the law, and it is with reference to the law that the agonizing dilemma arises, expressed in the words: 'Wretched man that I am! Who will deliver me from this body of death?' Paul has been saying that in Christ we are dead to the law, just as we are dead to sin in Him, and the question now is: 'Is the law sin, that we need to be set free from it?'

In answering this question the apostle leads us into what is certainly one of the most complex and controversial problems in biblical interpretation. As a possible key to understanding, it is worth noting that in the earlier part of the chapter[6] the apostle speaks first of 'what we were' — 'while we were living in the flesh, our sinful passions, aroused by the law, were at work in our members to bear fruit for death' — and then of 'what we are' — 'but now we are discharged from the law, dead to that which held us captive, so that we serve not under the old written code but in the new life of the

[6] Rom. 7:5, 6.

Spirit.' This contrast seems to be maintained throughout the remainder of the chapter, with verses 7-13 reflecting the former, and verses 14-25 the latter.

Law exposes sin

Paul's argument, then, in the first of these two sections is this: The answer to the question 'Is the law sin?' is in the negative. The law is not sinful, but it is the revealer of sin. A man does not know the power of sin in his life until the law comes in with its sanctions. Until it did, sin was dead in Paul's life, *i.e.* it was not felt by him in its malignant power, but was lying dormant. But when the law came, it was aroused into activity (a truth demonstrated by the fact that being forbidden something generally makes a man covet it all the more). Sin thus takes the law into its service, as it were, and uses it for its own evil purposes. As the apostle says elsewhere,[7] 'the power of sin is the law.' In this respect the law becomes a destroying power. But it was not originally intended to be so. Its primary aim was to make men responsive to the will of God by revealing that will to them, for it is the expression of the character of God. But it *becomes* a very different thing because of sin, and because sin finds opportunity through it.

It is this ambiguous character of the law that Paul echoes again later in the Epistle[8] when he speaks of 'what the law, weakened by the flesh, could not do' — *i.e.* make men responsive to the divine will, which was its *original* function. Thus the law becomes, through sin, something which in its own nature it is not, a destroying power, and it is from this that we are set free by Christ in

[7] 1 Cor. 15:56. [8] Rom. 8:3.

the gospel. Not that something that is ordained by God is made death to us; it is rather that sin makes use of the law and puts it to evil ends. But God in the end ' turns the tables ' on sin, for although sin makes use of God's good law to work evil in us, He also makes use of what sin does in us through the law to show us sin in all its ugliness and sinfulness, thus bringing us to a deeper realization of our need of Christ.[9]

Normal Christian experience?

Controversy reaches its height, however, in the second section of the passage,[1] and widely differing opinions are held as to interpretation. Does what Paul says refer to a believer looking back on his unconverted days, or to a believer's experience when he is living a defeated life, or to normal Christian experience? All these questions have been answered in the affirmative; but if we recall that at this point the apostle changes from the past to the present tense, the reasonable conclusion is that he is speaking of something in his present experience. This is objected to on the ground that it puts a low estimate on the power of grace to give victory in the Christian life, and the words ' I am carnal, sold under sin '[2] are quoted to substantiate the claim that Paul cannot be speaking of *normal* Christian experience. But the Greek word here does not mean ' carnally minded '. There are two words in the original, both translated ' carnal ' in the AV but having different meanings, *sarkikos* and *sarkinos*. The first of these does refer to ' carnal minded-

[9] This, in the main, is the interpretation given by Anders Nygren in his *Commentary on Romans*. The whole passage owes much to the insight he gives there.

[1] Rom. 7:14-25. [2] Rom. 7:14.

ness ', but the second — and it is this that Paul uses here — refers simply to the fact that he is still ' in the flesh ', even as a Christian, and therefore participates in its limitations. The Christian is called to live his new life in the old death-doomed environment. He is thus in a paradoxical position, being both ' free from sin ' and at the same time ' subject to the condition of sin '. Because he is both ' in Christ ' and ' in the flesh ' he is not able to be a sinner, and since this is so, there will always be tension and conflict in his experience.

This has already been referred to earlier,[3] and it also appears in the magnificent eighth chapter, which, above all, describes Christian victory in the life of the Spirit. There, in the midst of such phrases as, ' The law of the Spirit of life in Christ Jesus has set me free ',[4] and ' the glorious liberty of the children of God ',[5] he can also say, ' We . . . groan . . . as we wait for adoption . . .'[6] — a thought he echoes elsewhere in his Epistles.[7] It is this ' groan ' that is expressed in the despairing cry, ' Wretched man that I am! Who will deliver me from this body of death? '[8] In Christ the Christian is free from sin, yet, paradoxically, sin has not yet vanished from his life, and the will to do right is often in conflict with the inability to perform it![9] As Paul puts it elsewhere: ' For the desires of the flesh are against the Spirit, and the desires of the Spirit are against the flesh; for these are opposed to each other, to prevent you from doing what you would.'[1] It is not always realized that this interpretation is the only logical alternative to the claim to sinless perfection, which, as we have already seen, was certainly not in the apostle's mind.

[3] Rom. 6; see p. 40. [4] Rom. 8:2. [5] Rom. 8:21.
[6] Rom. 8:23. [7] 2 Cor. 5:4. [8] Rom. 7:24.
[9] Rom. 7:19. [1] Gal. 5:17.

The fact of Satan

There are still, however, two further points to be underlined. The first is that twice the apostle uses the phrase, 'it is no longer I that do it, but sin which dwells within me.'[2] This is a very startling thing to say, and it bears witness to the reality of what psychologists sometimes call a divided personality. Sanday and Headlam[3] say it is 'a further proof that the Power which exerts so baneful an influence is not merely an attribute of the man himself but has an objective existence'. Earlier, in reference to the phrase, 'I do not understand my own actions',[4] they make the comment, 'The man acts, so to speak, blindly; he is not a fully conscious agent; a force which he cannot resist takes the decision out of his hands.'[5]

It is difficult to avoid the impression that Paul is speaking of sin here almost as if it had a personality, and it is not surprising that some have thought that there is a satanic dimension indicated in the agonizing conflict which the apostle unfolds. Certainly he uses words descriptive of the reign of sin in human life that imply personality, particularly in the analogy of the two masters,[6] and part at least of the mystery expressed in this passage may surely be explained in terms of Satan working in our members, for his activities in the human spirit often take the form of compulsive actions — indeed, this is one of the surest ways of recognizing his presence, as, for example, in the plagues of unbidden and unwanted evil thoughts that sometimes bombard the mind. The whole question of the reality of the demonic

[2] Rom. 7:17, 20.
[3] *International Critical Commentary, Romans*, p. 182.
[4] Rom. 7:15. [5] *I.C.C., Romans*, p. 182. [6] Rom. 6:15-23.

element in spiritual experience, which J. S. Stewart has called 'a neglected element in New Testament theology', needs to be examined in this connection far more seriously and comprehensively than has yet been done. It must never be forgotten that, behind the outward conflict of the Christian, there is the unseen battle with principalities and powers. Paul's profound statement on this subject in the Epistle to the Ephesians[7] may yet be found to be the best and most penetrating commentary on the controversial seventh chapter of Romans.

The 'much more' of grace

The final point is this: we have interpreted this conflict as being an inevitable part of the Christian experience, and it may well be asked whether this does not paint the possibilities of Christian life in too sombre colours. Is this all that grace is able to do? The answer is that the tension between flesh and spirit is not an equal tension. The new life in Christ is incomparably greater and stronger than the old nature. This is Paul's whole point in the introductory paragraph to this section of the Roman Epistle.[8] There is the 'much more' of grace.[9] As Christians, and even within the limits of 'the flesh', we have the first-fruits of the Spirit, and this more than offsets the down-drag of the flesh. The 'reign in life'[1] is no fiction, but an indisputable fact, and there are very great possibilities of victory within the experience of the 'groaning'.[2] Particular sins, habits, attitudes, that used to cripple and paralyse life, will certainly yield to the power of

[7] Eph. 6:10-17. [8] Rom. 5:12-21. [9] Rom. 5:15, 17, 20.
[1] Rom. 5:17. [2] Rom. 8:23.

grace, but when all this is said — and it is not a small thing to say! — it is still true that we are not able *not* to be sinners, and therefore still in the position of having to cry, 'Wretched man that I am! Who will deliver me from this body of death?'[3]

Full deliverance is not yet: we are saved in hope.[4] There is a minor note in the music of the Christian life, but this minor motif is not the final movement of the divine symphony, but leads on to the glorious climax and consummation whose crashing chords and sonorous harmonies resolve all tensions and answer all questions. As Paul puts it elsewhere:[5] 'This slight momentary affliction is preparing for us an eternal weight of glory beyond all comparison.'

[3] Rom. 7:24. [4] Rom. 8:24. [5] 2 Cor. 4:17.

CHAPTER FOUR

The fight of faith

HAVING DEALT WITH our union with Christ in His death and resurrection as the new position God has given us through faith, and with the need for a true knowledge and understanding of what God has done for us and where He has placed us in Christ — the lack of which is one of the two major hindrances to spiritual life — we must now turn to a consideration of the response that requires to be made to the affirmations of the gospel. It has already been pointed out[1] that faith means to consider or 'reckon' ourselves 'dead to sin and alive to God',[2] and that faith in action is expressed in the words, 'Let not sin therefore reign in your mortal bodies . . . but yield yourselves to God as men who have been brought from death to life'[3]; that is to say, we are to recognize the facts of our position in Christ *to be* facts, and act upon them in such a way that the dominion of sin will be destroyed in our lives.[4] But this in itself raises issues that oblige us to consider more fully the precise nature of this 'reckoning', and in so doing we come to the second major hindrance to spiritual life, the lack of will and intention to submit to God.

[1] Chapter 2, pp. 35ff. [2] Rom. 6:11. [3] Rom. 6:12, 13.
[4] Rom. 6:14.

The response of faith

What does the apostle mean when he speaks of living ' by faith in the Son of God '?[5] This question may be answered by considering what he writes in the chapter already quoted: ' But thanks be to God, that you who were once slaves of sin have become obedient from the heart to the standard of teaching to which you were committed.'[6] We gather from this that faith is not merely an intellectual acceptance of the facts of our redemption, but also a moral submission to them. The gospel is something that must be obeyed from the heart. And this is the great stumbling-block: for we are not willing to submit to the facts of our salvation.

It is sometimes said of the gospel, ' It is a matter of simple faith ', and, rightly understood, this is true. It is open to question, however, whether the terrific challenge inherent in ' simple faith ' is always realized. 'All you have to do is believe ' is sometimes said to enquirers. But ' believing ' involves repentance, that is to say, dying to the old life, and obedience and surrender of the will to Christ. This is what it costs to ' believe ', and the cost of ' simple faith ' must likewise be read into any true understanding of what Paul means by ' reckoning '.[7]

The issue might be simply stated thus: our position in Christ is that we are united with Him in His death and resurrection. But it must become our possession also. Our death to sin in the death of Christ must become an experimental reality in our lives. It is, of course, the work of the Holy Spirit to make it so; it is He, as Lord and Giver of life, who makes real in us what Christ has wrought for us. But He works only when we yield ourselves to God in obedience and surrender. The

[5] Gal. 2:20. [6] Rom. 6:17. [7] Rom. 6:11, AV.

Holy Ghost is given, as Peter is careful to point out, to them that obey God.[8]

Our Lord's own words underline this point very clearly. God has incorporated us into Christ: that is our position. But we must abide in Him. And what is it to abide in Him but to obey Him? 'If you keep my commandments,' He said,[9] 'you will abide in my love.' And obedience to Him is to say in the spirit of Gethsemane, 'Not my will, but thine, be done';[1] that is, to deny oneself, and to die to the self-life which is the heart of all sin.

The moral challenge

This, then, is how Christian freedom and victory will become real in experience — by becoming 'obedient from the heart to the standard of teaching to which you were committed'.[2] Literally translated, Paul's words read: 'obeying from the heart the mould of teaching to which you were delivered.' The word in the Greek for 'form' or 'mould' is *typos*, and means the impress a die makes on a soft surface, or the mould into which molten metal is poured, and which gives shape to the metal when it is cooled. The 'teaching' of the Epistle to the Romans, Paul is saying, is the mould which is to 'shape' the life of the believer, and leave its mark upon him. Now, the 'shape' of the biblical teaching on sanctification is that of a cross, and if lives are to be sanctified, the marks of the cross will be reproduced in them.

It might be put this way: when the living truth of God touches a man, the impress that it makes upon him is

[8] Acts 5:32. [9] Jn. 15:10. [1] Lk. 22:42.
[2] See Rom. 6:17.

the mark of the cross. Nor has any man understood the gospel aright if he does not see it to mean that he is called to the obedience of faith; that is to say, to deny himself and take up the cross and follow Christ. To fail to give this meaning to faith is simply to deceive oneself.

It is precisely because this moral challenge is involved in the New Testament conception of faith that all the classical expressions of consecration and discipleship are given in terms of sacrifice and the note of suffering stressed — putting to death,[3] crucifying,[4] renouncing,[5] taking up the cross.[6] In one of the most characteristic utterances of all, Paul says, 'I appeal to you therefore, brethren, by the mercies of God, to present your bodies as a living sacrifice',[7] a sentiment borne out to the full in his own experience, as is seen in the following words: 'I count everything as loss because of the surpassing worth of knowing Christ Jesus my Lord. For his sake I have suffered the loss of all things, and count them as refuse, in order that I may gain Christ . . .'[8] Nothing could demonstrate more clearly that it is in the obedience we offer to the summons of the gospel that faith is proved real and that we experience the liberating power of the Holy Spirit in our personal lives, and His enduement for service.

It is here, then, that the crux of the whole matter lies, for, deep down, we do not really wish to obey in this total sense. We do not really want to die — we want to live 'for ourselves'.[9] Christ's words, 'If any man would come after me, let him deny himself and take up his cross and follow me',[1] crystallize the challenge of

[3] Rom. 8:13. [4] Gal. 5:24. [5] Tit. 2:12.
[6] Mk. 8:34. [7] Rom. 12:1. [8] Phil. 3:8.
[9] *Cf.* 2 Cor. 5:15. [1] Mt. 16:24.

consecration; they tell us that we must die, and until we do, we cannot live the life of victory.

The real nature of sin

Something further needs to be said, however, in this connection. When Paul speaks of ' becoming obedient from the heart ', he means ' obedience at the heart of one's being ', and this obliges us to consider what is the real nature of the bondage under which we are held as sinners. In view of the widespread misunderstanding of what the Scriptures mean by sin, it is necessary to deal with this question in some detail.

The first thing that must be noted is that it is not a sufficient diagnosis of the problem to pin-point any particular sin. It is true, of course, that a particular sin may be a major problem, and the words of Tersteegen's well-known hymn:

> ' Is there a thing beneath the sun
> That strives with Thee my heart to share?
> Ah! tear it thence, and reign alone,
> The Lord of every motion there '

may express only too clearly the inner disorder in the life of an individual. Some habit or relationship may grip the spiritual life, making it barren and ineffectual; worldly things, worldly considerations, worldly interests and people, battle for the allegiance of our hearts day by day, and there is nothing quite so sad as to see the shadow of the world come over a Christian's life, and to see him gradually, steadily, imperceptibly, being beguiled from the simplicity that is in Christ, and losing the fine edge of his consecration.

But this is merely symptomatic of a still deeper problem, and must not be mistaken for the disease itself. Nor is it sufficient to think in terms of the more inward sins of the spirit — pride, ambition, envy, malice — which may corrode the heart and mar the testimony of the believer long after the question of outward worldliness has been left behind. That these are frequently problems in the Christian church cannot be doubted; they were, for example, in the fellowship of believers in Corinth, where, in spite of the pre-eminent gifts they had, and potential for God, everything was marred by the factions and divisions that existed among them, and by the unholy spirit of ambition that made some of them, such as Diotrephes,[2] love to have the preeminence.

It is obvious that competitive claims in the life, worldly considerations, evil passions, constitute a grave and urgent concern in the life of the believer. But none of these, either singly or together, brings us to the heart of the biblical insight into the nature of sin, and the danger lies in stopping short and failing to realize that the real situation is still more critical and urgent. For these are symptoms, and only symptoms, of something that lies much deeper, and, until this is realized, we may fall into the error of exchanging one set of sins for another, and mistaking this for deliverance. It is a supreme tragedy — and very frightening — when a man, under the impression that he is being saved from sin, merely alters the pattern of sin in his life, from the less respectable and more obvious, to the less obvious and more respectable. The evil one is well satisfied to bring about such a deception.

[2] 3 Jn. 9.

Enthronement of self

An example of this very danger is seen in our Lord's story about the Pharisee and the publican.[3] The Pharisee's religious record is an impressive one — let this at once be conceded and honour given where it is due — and there were no obvious marks of worldliness in his life. But the real force of the parable lies in the exposure of the complete self-centredness of his life, religious though it was. It is his self-consciousness and self-absorption that obtrude throughout. The real problem of his life had never been touched; self was deeply entrenched and reigning supreme.

It is here that the heart of the matter lies. The essence of sin is not that we do this or that which is evil; it is that within each of us which clamours: 'my desires must be satisfied, my lusts must be gratified, my way must be taken, my will must be done.' It is certain that, with some, this will take the form of worldliness, with some it will lead to immorality and profligacy, but with others it may well be much more subtle and less obvious, especially if, as in the case of the Pharisee, it has a veneer of religion. But ultimately, whether we are beset by this particular sin or that becomes relatively unimportant in face of this terrible, all-devouring appetite within us which is the root and cause of all sins.

As William Temple, late Archbishop of Canterbury, once put it: 'A great deal too much attention has been given to sins as compared with sin. And so if it happens that I cannot think of any particular wrong thing I have done, or any particular right thing I might have done and neglected, yet still I must ask God to be merciful to

[3] Lk. 18:9ff.

me a sinner, for I share the common sin of mankind, and make myself in a host of ways the centre of the world. I think like a man, and not like God.'

Self the centre

'I make myself . . . the centre of the world.' This is the meaning of sin. And it is one of Satan's chief wiles to make the believer obsessed with what, by comparison, are mere peccadilloes in his experience, and remain all the while unaware and ignorant of the real issues. The Scriptures give us ample evidence of this sinister reality. In the story of the rich fool,[4] for example, there is no reference to specific sins at all. The man was not dishonest. No charge of evil living is brought against him. There is no suggestion of unscrupulous dealings in business. What we are meant to see is the chronic self-centredness of the life he lived. No-one was allowed to break into the isolation with which he surrounded himself. He locked himself into a little world of his own, and never at any time did he escape from himself. He was immersed in a constant pre-occupation with his own concerns. He was the centre of his own existence, and nothing in all his experience was half so important as himself. He had never seriously thought of anyone else.

The story of the prodigal son[5] affords another illustration quite as graphic as the former. He could certainly be described as a wayward and easily-led boy, impressionable, impetuous and foolhardy, but none of these descriptions touches the real problem of his life. It is in the words he spoke to his father before he left home on his disastrous course that the real clue to his

[4] Lk. 12:16-20. [5] Lk. 15:11-32.

predicament is given. He said: '*Give me* the share of property that falls to me.'[6] He made himself the centre of his world, and it was from this that all his prodigal living issued.

The uncrucified self

It is this central citadel at the heart of our being, inverted and perverted against God as it is, that is the heart of sin. And worldliness, carnality, impurity, unhallowed relationships and the like derive their seriousness from the fact that they are simply expressions of this evil root, this horrid, voracious thing that is black as hell itself. We must learn to trace our crying sins back to their proper source and see whence they spring. Sin expresses itself in all manner of subtleties, and perhaps especially in the religious life. It is there that it takes up its final stronghold, thinking to conceal itself with impunity. It is often true that beneath the deep earnestness and intensity of a Christian's life there is a self that is uncrucified, and a death he has refused to die.

This could scarcely be underlined more graphically than is done in the following words from an unknown source:[7] 'The last enemy to be destroyed in the believer is self. It dies hard. It will make any concessions, if only it is allowed to live. Self will permit the believer to do anything, give anything, sacrifice anything, suffer anything, go anywhere, take any liberties, bear any crosses, afflict soul and body to any degree — anything, if it can only live. It will consent to live in a hovel, in a garret, in the slums, in far away

[6] Lk. 15:12.
[7] Quoted by L. E. Maxwell, in *Born Crucified.*

heathendom, if only its life can be spared.' Martin Luther used to say: 'I am more afraid of my own heart than of the pope and all his cardinals. I have within me that great pope, Self.' The words of Cowper's hymn:

> 'The dearest idol I have known,
>   Whate'er that idol be,
> Help me to tear it from Thy throne,
>   And worship only Thee'

searching and challenging as they are, sometimes tend to focus attention upon some specific sin, and obscure the fact that the greatest idol in any man's experience is self, and that it is this that must be torn from the throne, so as to give Christ His rightful place in the life.

The writer once heard two speakers preaching on this theme. The first spoke of Abraham and Isaac, and roundly challenged his congregation with the necessity of laying their dearest on earth on the altar for God. The second, however, touched a deeper note, for he said, in effect, 'God does not want your Isaac; He wants *you.*' This is the real issue. It is possible to lay one's Isaac on the altar, however dear and precious, instead of yielding the self to God, and we must be careful lest well-meaning but biblically-defective presentations of the challenge to consecration beguile us and hide from us the true 'self-destroying' discipline of the cross. Only when, with Paul, we can say of our Christian lives, 'No longer I',[8] have we truly understood what the Bible means by sin and the deliverance from it that the gospel brings.

[8] Gal. 2:20.

The self-denial of Christ

Our Lord's teaching at Caesarea Philippi[9] and His dealings with the disciples assume a new and deeper significance when viewed in the light of this fundamental analysis. His words: 'If any man would come after me, let him deny himself and take up his cross and follow me'[1] are so well known that their force is sometimes missed. It is not always realized that in what follows — the story of the transfiguration[2] — Christ gives a very practical illustration of what these words mean; for the central focus of the mystery of the transfiguration experience was 'his departure, which he was to accomplish at Jerusalem',[3] and He came down from the glory of the mountain experience, turned His back upon it, and steadfastly set His face to go to Jerusalem.[4] As Paul puts it, 'Christ did not please himself.'[5] He denied Himself, and came down — into death.

The contrast between His attitude and that of His disciples is complete. At Caesarea Philippi Peter baulked at the message of the cross. This is made very plain in the record.[6] The strength and swiftness of our Lord's rebuke to him is quite unmistakable. He would brook no kind of discipleship without a cross, and attributed the very suggestion of it to Satan.

A little later, when they came to Capernaum,[7] Jesus asked them, 'What were you discussing on the way?' The significance of this question should not be missed. Having listened to the solemn, heart-searching words of the Son of God about the death He was about to die, having seen His glory on the mount, these men were actually wrangling and bickering among themselves,

[9] Mk. 8:34-38. [1] Mk. 8:34. [2] Mk. 9:1-9. [3] Lk. 9:31.
[4] Lk. 9:51. [5] Rom. 15:3. [6] Mk. 8:31-33. [7] Mk. 9:33ff.

jockeying for position in the disciple band! Such was the state of their hearts. And they had asked Jesus concerning their failure to help the distracted father of the demon-possessed boy, 'Why could not we cast it out?'[8] Why indeed! It was because they were the kind of men they were. Matthew states explicitly in his version of the incident[9] that Jesus replied, 'Because of your unbelief.'

The moral issue

But unbelief is not an intellectual problem only; it is also a moral one. The disciples did not have faith to cast the demon out because they had not submitted themselves to the discipline of the cross, nor allowed it to deal with their unhallowed motives and intentions, these stirrings of ambition in their hearts. There was a death they had refused to die, and consequently their faith did not work. For faith that casts out demons lies on the other side of death. It was our Lord's own unwavering adherence to the principle of the cross, shown here in His coming down from the mount, that explains His power to bless, and heal, and save.

The root cause of failure

The question, 'Why could not we cast him out?' is one that has relevance for the church today and needs to be asked in all honesty as we face the spiritual problems of our corporate life, in congregation or Christian organization. The problems of communication, the drift from the churches, the ineffectiveness of our evangelism and outreach, the low ebb of our spiritual life, the

[8] Mk. 9:28. [9] Mt. 17:20, AV.

barrenness and unfruitfulness of so many ministries, the lack of spiritual unction, even where orthodoxy in theology cannot be called in question — all alike may have at their root this refusal of the discipline of the cross, and of the death that brings life. Even in the context of that bitter cry, 'Wretched man that I am! Who will deliver me from this body of death?'[1] we must still ask ourselves whether part of our heart does not have a secret sympathy for sin and a secret hankering after it. It is so often true of us that we do not really want to die. Part of us wants the cursed thing. It is there, at that point, that the crux of the matter lies; there the axe must be laid at the root of the tree.

It was because Peter was so loath to come to this point that he ultimately denied Christ. It was inevitable that he should have done so, for it was the logical outcome of his refusal to die. There is a strange irony in the words he spoke in this connection, prior to, and at, the denial. On the night on which Jesus was betrayed, he protested with great vehemence, 'Even if I must die with you, I will not deny you.'[2] And at the denial itself, he expostulated, 'I do not know the man.'[3] In a sense far other than he intended, these words express the simple truth about himself. Peter did not in fact know Christ with the kind of knowledge that keeps men from denying Him. For this knowledge lies on the other side of death. We must, as Paul points out, count all things loss — that is, we must die, that we may know Him and the power of His resurrection.[4] Thus, when we read his protestation, 'Even if I must die with you . . .', we cannot but think in our hearts: 'If only you had, Peter, in the true spiritual sense, you would not have denied Christ.'

[1] Rom. 7:24. [2] Mt. 26:35. [3] Mt. 26:74. [4] Phil. 3:8, 10.

It is in the light of this moral breakdown that we can best understand the encounter Peter had with the risen Christ on the shore of Galilee,[5] when the Lord penetratingly asked him, 'Simon, son of John, do you love me?' It is well known that in the original Greek Jesus used a different word for 'love' from that which figures in Peter's reply. We may distinguish these two words fairly by saying that Peter's word placed his love for Christ in the realm of the natural affections, whereas Christ's word spoke of a love that involved the will. What, in effect, He said to Peter was: 'Does your love for Me constrain you to yield your will to Me? Do you love Me unto death?' That is the point. And at last, the ploughshare of the cross seems to have touched his inmost heart and life. It is significant that Peter's First Epistle is shot through and through with the reality of the challenge of the cross and the duty and privilege laid on believers of sharing Christ's sufferings.

Dying to live

This, then, is the great pattern unfolded in the Scriptures: we *die* to *live*; but life, not death, is the true goal of sacrifice (and this is true both for personal life and for Christian service). As the apostle puts it, 'So death is at work in us, but life in you.'[6] Reference has already been made to Luke's account of the transfiguration story[7] in which he refers to Moses and Elijah speaking with Christ 'of his departure, which he was to accomplish at Jerusalem', and this also gives a remarkable illustration of the paradoxical 'death-life' principle, which has been called the law of spiritual harvest. The word translated 'departure', referring to

[5] Jn. 21:15ff. [6] 2 Cor. 4:12. [7] Lk. 9:28; see p. 61.

Christ's death on the cross, is *exodos* which means 'a way out'. For Christ, the cross was 'a way out' of constraint into world blessing. 'I have a baptism to be baptized with', He once said, 'and how I am constrained until it is accomplished!'[8] He knew that the purpose for which He had come into the world could not be fulfilled until He had experienced the fiery baptism of His passion.

The experience of the cross is in the same way 'a way out' for all who follow Him. When He challenges us to take up the cross, He is saying, in effect, 'Behold, I have set before you an open door'.[9] The real reason for our ineffectiveness is to be sought, not in any technical problems of communication, but in the fact that there is a baptism that we have yet to be baptized with, a baptism of total obedience from the heart. This is the one effective 'way out' into the glorious liberty of the children of God.

Jesus Christ is Lord

There remains one further word to be said at this point. It is that the claim of Christ is a total one, and this is involved and implied in the recognition of who He is. For this Christ who lives in us — in all His greatness and glory, pity and compassion — is God the Lord; He is the rightful King and liege Lord of our lives, who claims us utterly for Himself, and summons us inexorably to discipleship. The inspiration of knowing the nature of the indwelling Christ carries with it a tremendous challenge, and He always meant His gospel to be understood in this way, as is clear from the testimony borne to Him by the writers of the Gospels. The whole structure of the

[8] Lk. 12:50. [9] Rev. 3:8.

Gospels bears evidence of this, for the Evangelists are obviously intent upon demonstrating the Lordship of Christ in all its aspects.

The record of the miracles is given with this in view, and Christ is shown as Lord of nature, stilling storms, turning water into wine, multiplying the loaves and fishes; as Lord of disease, in the many healings of sick and broken bodies and minds; as Lord of demons, when they cowered before Him and were not suffered to bear testimony to Him; as Lord of death itself, when the king of terrors took marching orders at His mighty word; as Lord of men, in the way in which He commanded their absolute devotion and allegiance.

The aim is uniform throughout: it is to show that obedience is not optional for those who would follow Him. He *requires* us to obey Him. The old phrase, once much used and well known in another connection in the life of the Scottish church, 'the crown rights of the Redeemer', is one that properly expresses what the Scriptures claim for Him. He is a King, and He has crown rights in our lives. The question is: Do we acknowledge His Lordship and Kingship? If we do we must bow the knee before Him, and crown Him Lord of all.

This is what faith means: to be captured and mastered by Christ.

CHAPTER FIVE

Crisis or process?

SOME FURTHER QUESTIONS in connection with faith's response to the summons of the gospel remain to be considered, and these must now be dealt with in order to prevent the possibility of serious misunderstanding.

It has been thought, for example, that in speaking of being crucified with Christ, Paul is referring to something that happens 'once for all' in the experience of the believer, as if that were the end of the matter. This, however, is not the case. It is true, as Calvin points out, that when the apostle says, 'Likewise reckon ye also yourselves to be dead indeed unto sin, but alive unto God through Jesus Christ our Lord,'[1] the force of the word 'likewise' is that it refers to His having died to sin 'once for all'[2] (*hapax*) and that the believer's 'reckoning' partakes of this 'once for all' nature — that is to say, he may properly be said to die once for all in the sense that he is reconciled to God by the blood of Christ, and regenerated by His Spirit into newness of life.

But faith, properly understood, is both an act and an attitude, and the 'once for all' experience of the believer must be implemented by the adoption of a

[1] Rom. 6:11, AV. [2] See Rom. 6:10.

principle of living in which personal crucifixion is the abiding characteristic. Obviously the new life must have a beginning sometime, but *in the experience of the believer* it may begin suddenly, in a crisis, or alternatively it may develop only gradually, through a progressive and deepening understanding of the truth.

'Death' principle the rule of life

But whether crisis or process, the all-important reality is the adoption of the 'death' principle as the rule of life. Thus Paul can use phrases such as 'I die every day',[3] 'always carrying in the body the death of Jesus',[4] to describe his spiritual experience.

It is recorded of William Booth, the founder of the Salvation Army, that, when asked what was the secret of his outstanding fruitfulness as a Christian leader, he replied: 'I determined as a lad of sixteen that God was going to have all that there was of William Booth.' These words express very plainly both a once-for-all determination to consecrate himself utterly to God, and also the adoption of a principle for living which continued throughout his whole ministry.

That act and attitude necessarily go together may also be seen in the experience of the apostle Peter. Reference has already been made to the 'death-life' pattern which began to operate in him after his encounter with the risen Christ,[5] and the events of the Day of Pentecost may fairly be said to be concrete evidence of its reality. But there were other 'deaths' that Peter had to die, and from the sacred record it is clear that he was not always willing to do so, even within the context of the Pentecostal outpouring of the Spirit of God. One

[3] 1 Cor. 15:31. [4] 2 Cor. 4:10. [5] Jn. 21:15-22.

thinks, for example, of how slow he was to concede the possibility of the admission of the Gentiles to participation in the blessings of the gospel. Basically this can be understood only as an unwillingness to die to his deeply-ingrained prejudices as an orthodox Jew. It took a special dispensation from God in the form of a miraculous vision[6] to convince him, and even then he gave but tardy recognition to the Gentiles' claims.[7]

In this connection it is interesting and significant that some time later, when Paul visited Jerusalem,[8] he was obliged to rebuke Peter openly on the matter of his attitude to the Gentile believers. The heart of this situation was simply that Peter had compromised himself for fear of the Jews, and had departed from the position he had adopted in the household of Cornelius,[9] a position he knew to be right, and for the time being took lower ground. Used and owned of God as undoubtedly he had been, he departed from the place of obedience, and had to be challenged by Paul to die a new 'death' for the gospel's sake. From which we may learn that there is no place of spiritual advancement or attainment a believer can reach from which it is not possible to fall away.

The battle for sanctification

But this implies a continual watchfulness in the spiritual life and leads to the consideration of a further possible misunderstanding. It may be asked, 'If sanctification is by faith, as seems to be implied in what has been maintained in the exposition of Paul's teaching in the Epistle to the Romans, then what is to be the interpre-

[6] Acts 10:9ff. [7] Acts 10:28, 29. [8] Gal. 2:11.
[9] Acts 10.

tation of all that the New Testament teaches about battling and wrestling in the Christian life?'

In answering this question it should not be forgotten that the New Testament itself significantly links together these two seemingly contradictory ideas in one of its most characteristic phrases, the 'fight of faith'.[1] This should serve as a reminder that there is no real contradiction between the two in the thought of the New Testament itself.

There must, however, be a clear understanding of the phraseology that is used in this debate. The words, for example, of the hymn,

> 'Holiness by faith in Jesus
> Not by effort of my own'

are deceptively simple and unequivocal, but a great deal depends on the meaning that is given to them. If what is meant is a simple 'believing' unrelated to the fight of faith, then this is at variance with the teaching of the New Testament as a whole. It must be insisted, on biblical grounds, that there is no experience in the life of the believer that can ever dispense with the discipline and effort of the Christian life, and it is extremely misleading, and productive of a good deal of confusion, to suggest that there is. The answer lies in an understanding of what is meant by 'simple faith', which has already[2] been seen to involve a costly heart obedience. One has only to think of the battles that have to be fought in the soul in order to maintain a constant attitude of obedience to the will of God, to realize that battles and wrestlings stand in no kind of contradiction to true faith.

[1] 1 Tim. 6:12, AV. [2] See p. 52.

The ' fight ' of faith not a struggle

On the other hand, the meaning of the ' fight ' of faith must not be confused with the struggle, often marked by failure, which characterizes many Christian lives, a struggle which ought not to be, and need not be. There is, however, a struggle which is the indispensable hallmark of the believer's life, and one to which he is necessarily committed.

A simple illustration will suffice to distinguish between the two. A prisoner may struggle unavailingly to set himself free from the chains that bind him, for they are too powerful for him, and his jailer mocks at his helpless efforts. This is the picture of the struggle that ought not to be, and need not be, in a believer's life. But the prisoner may be set free, and the chains that bind him may be broken. Then he is free to fight again, and to do battle against his captors, which he may do to some purpose. This also is a parable of the believer's life. It is only when he is set free that he can engage the enemy in the Lord's name. And when he does, it is a fierce and enduring battle to which he is committed, and there may be many wounds. But he is no longer battling to be free, he battles from a position of freedom, and indeed, is able to battle only because he is free.

To change the metaphor, one may think of a drowning man's reaction when a good swimmer plunges into the water to attempt his rescue. His panicking efforts to help himself actually hinder the rescue operation. He must stop struggling to help himself and leave himself entirely in the hands of his rescuer. He must simply allow himself to be saved from drowning. But the battle he has, morally and physically, to stop struggling may be a terrific one, and in the compass of a few brief moments he may die a thousand deaths, in keeping still and trusting himself to his rescuer. But this is surely a different struggle from the other, and a necessary one.

So it is in the spiritual life. To change over from one's own feeble, unavailing struggles to set oneself free from sin, to the reckoning of faith, and to maintain such reckoning, is a battle of the greatest magnitude, and explains why Paul speaks of it in terms of fighting the good fight of faith, and holding the faith. The fight of faith is, in fact, very often a fight for faith.

Scripture, not experience, the criterion

There is, however, another and still more widespread confusion of thought. There are those who not only assert the 'once-for-all' nature of our dying with Christ, but do so in terms of a necessary crisis in the life of the believer. They are certain that sanctification involves a crisis, because they themselves have had a crisis in their experience, and therefore it must be so. But there is a wrong principle at work in this form of reasoning. What happens is that they begin with their experience of crisis — one does not doubt its reality or validity — and proceed to interpret the Scriptures in the light of it. But this is not a procedure that is permitted to the believer. On the contrary, he must begin with the Scriptures, and interpret experience in their light. To fail to do so is to fall into all kinds of extravagant error.

Those who begin with experience and interpret the Scriptures in the light of it tend to speak of conversion as one stage for the believer, and consecration, or sanctification, as another, on the grounds that they themselves have had a post-conversion experience of consecration which has been far more significant and definitive for their Christian life than the initial one of conversion. Indeed, certain terminology may be used to describe this further stage — the baptism of the Spirit, a second work of grace, and other such terms. But if we begin with the Scriptures, a very different picture emerges. We do not, of course, doubt the validity of these experiences, but take leave to call in question the interpretation of them.

The Scriptures do not, in fact, teach a second work of grace, except as a continuing work in the life of the believer. According to the Scriptures, conversion and consecration are simultaneous, in the sense that no conversion ever really takes place that does not mean, imply and involve a true consecration to Christ. One does not give part of one's allegiance to Christ at conversion, then at a later stage make a complete surrender to Him, called consecration. One does not enter into the kingdom at all except on terms of unconditional surrender. This, in fact, is what conversion means, and should be clear from what has already been said about Paul's teaching on the subject.[3] It is surely obvious that, so far as the apostle was concerned, 'believing unto justification' implies and involves a total surrender of all our sinful ways. To repent, to die to sin — these are in essence total, not partial, concepts.

Consecration and reconsecration

But — and this is important — a believer may lose the keen edge of his consecration and fall away from that attitude of total commitment which marked his entrance

[3] Rom. 6; see pp. 53f.

into the kingdom of God. If he does so, then a new consecration is necessary, and sometimes this is quite as clear-cut and decisive — and sudden — as a conversion experience, a crisis indeed, if this is the word to be used to describe it.

But it is necessary to be clear about what has happened. It is not an advance to another stage of experience so much as a return to a previous one. A great deal depends on a true realization of this. For obviously, if a believer does not fall away from his first consecration, but follows on to know the Lord ever more deeply, he does not require to renew it again (except in so far as our consecration is renewed day by day, and hour by hour, which is not the point at issue here).

Threefold function of the Word

Now the ministry of the Word may be said to have a threefold function and end in view; it can be illuminative, in that it enlightens the minds of those who are ignorant or confused in their understanding of the gospel; it can be therapeutic, in that it is medicine for those who are spiritually sick; it can be edifying, in that it provides food for those who are spiritually healthy and growing in the spiritual life. It is certainly true that spiritual illumination can take place suddenly. ' I see it now,' a man may cry, as the truth comes to him with all the force of a new revelation, and from that point onwards there is a marked difference in his life. A crisis has come, so to speak, in his spiritual thinking. It is true in the same way that a crisis can take place when the action of the Word on a man's soul is therapeutic, in the sense that it comes to convict and challenge him concerning things that ought not to be in his life. The pressure of the Word and Spirit of God may be such that a crisis — involving a specific thing or person — is precipitated in his heart. If a forbidden thing has soiled and marred his spiritual experience, it is very likely in fact that a crisis will arise, such as is implied in the words already quoted:[4]

'The dearest idol I have known,
Whate'er that idol be,
Help me to tear it from Thy throne,
And worship only Thee.'

Jesus said: 'If your right hand causes you to sin, cut it off.'[5] That is crisis enough in the believer's experience, in that it demands drastic action to put matters right, just as, in the sphere of medicine, appendicitis is a 'crisis' requiring immediate surgical intervention to safeguard life and health. But this drastic 'crisis-action' in the spiritual realm is therapeutic, and in one very important sense only preparatory to the real business of Christian growth. It removes the hindrance to growth and makes it possible, but it is not the growth itself, just as surgery removes the cause of illness and makes possible better health in the future.

Advancement in the spiritual life

If a man undergoes a crisis in his spiritual experience, this is likely to be what has happened to him. We should be glad, of course; but we must not misunderstand or misinterpret it, or confuse it to mean that, spiritually speaking, he has 'arrived'. On the contrary, he has only now set out on the real road of

[4] William Cowper; see p. 60. [5] Mt. 5:30.

advance. Now he can begin to grow, when the hindrances have been removed. But to insist, as is sometimes done, that every believer must have a crisis experience before he can know the fullness of God in his life is as misleading and erroneous as to say that everyone must have his appendix removed before true health is possible. A man who has not slipped back from his first consecration, but has progressed steadily in the spiritual life, does not need the therapy of the Word in this sense, but its nourishment to build him up and lead him on to maturity. The therapy of the Word merely brings us to the point where new life and development are possible, and this is the beginning, not the goal, of true spiritual life.

Real, effectual Christian experience, it must be insisted, does not begin properly until the believer comes to the obedience of faith in terms of total consecration to Christ. This needs to be underlined in a time when it is all too readily assumed, and taught, that Christians should be striving towards consecration of life as an ideal, or goal, instead of beginning from it as a base, as did all the heroes of faith whose lives are recorded in the Scriptures.[6] Abraham did not aspire to obedience; he began with it,[7] and nothing else can explain the vitality of his walk with God. From the outset Daniel 'resolved that he would not defile himself with the king's rich food',[8] and this alone accounts for the undeviating faithfulness of his witness throughout a long and testing experience.

It is in relation to the growth and development of Christian experience, when this 'death-principle' which is the heart of consecration has been entrenched and established as a reality in the life of the believer,

[6] See Heb. 11. [7] Heb. 11:8. [8] Dn. 1:8.

that the outworking of the doctrine of union with Christ is seen to be the dynamic of Christian living, and the one effectual enduement for service, and it is to this that we now turn in the next, and final, chapter.

CHAPTER SIX

Spiritual maturity

OUR FINAL CONSIDERATION of the doctrine of union with Christ must be its practical expression in daily living. The apostle Paul speaks of 'the life I now live in the flesh',[1] which, for him, meant a life into which God had wrought, by His Spirit, all the virtue of the work of Christ for men. The practical importance of this may be judged by the realization that the nature of the life a man lives determines the quality of the service he gives to Christ in the gospel, and ultimately the reward he receives at the last.[2] What is central in the kingdom of God is not so much what a man does, as what he is, namely his Christian character, and this, as we have seen, is something that grows and develops on the other side of the cross.

The ministry of edification

When the ministry of the Word has enlightened the ignorance and confusion in a man's mind, and led him into a true understanding of the doctrine of his union with Christ in His death and resurrection (the 'illuminative' function of the Word), and when it has

[1] Gal. 2:20. [2] Mt. 25:21, 23.

brought him to the place of moral submission, at whatever cost, to what it has made plain to him (its 'therapeutic' value) — that is to say, to the place where death 'works' in him to produce newness of life[3] — he is then in a position to receive its 'proper' ministry, which is for the upbuilding of the Christian. It is only when confusion is cleared away from the mind, and unwillingness to obey the will of God dealt with, that steady, healthy growth in spiritual life is possible. The lineaments of Christian character and stature, evidence of the believer's re-creation in Christ, will then begin to appear, as he proceeds to 'grow up in every way into him'.[4]

Giving gifts to men

This theme is expounded in some detail in the Epistle to the Ephesians in a passage remarkable for its range of thought and the graphic nature of its metaphors:

> 'Therefore it is said,
>
> "When he ascended on high he led
> a host of captives,
> and he gave gifts to men."
>
> . . . And his gifts were that some should be apostles, some prophets, some evangelists, some pastors and teachers, for the equipment of the saints, for the work of ministry, for building up the body of Christ, until we all attain to the unity of the faith and of the knowledge of the Son of God, to mature manhood, to the measure of the stature of the fullness of Christ; so that we may no longer be children, tossed

[3] See 2 Cor. 4:11. [4] Eph. 4:15.

to and fro and carried about with every wind of doctrine, by the cunning of men, by their craftiness in deceitful wiles. Rather, speaking the truth in love, we are to grow up in every way into him who is the head, into Christ, from whom the whole body, joined and knit together by every joint with which it is supplied, when each part is working properly, makes bodily growth and upbuilds itself in love.'[5]

At the heart of this passage, and underlying all its teaching, is the reality of the risen victorious Lord; and the gifts given by Him to the church are given on the basis, and as the fruit, of His ascension. This is the picture of the activity of a glorified and exalted Christ on the initiative to bless and sanctify His people. One is reminded of the parable which speaks of first binding the strong man and then plundering his house.[6] This is how the apostle thinks of the redemptive work of Christ: the victory over the powers of darkness in His death and resurrection, followed by the unloosing of the shackles, and the healing of the wounds and scars that the dark bondage of sin has inflicted upon their prey, and their restoration to freedom and personality once again. This He does by the institution of apostles, prophets, evangelists, pastors and teachers. It is through the ministry of the Word that the great work of rehabilitation is accomplished.

The equipment of the saints

The nature of this work is expressed in detail by Paul as being (in the New English Bible), 'to equip God's people for work in his service, to the building up of the body of Christ'.[7] The rendering given in the Revised

[5] Eph. 4:8-16. [6] Mk. 3:27. [7] Eph. 4:12.

Standard Version, giving a threefold division of the verse, is open to question, and the New English Bible translation, dividing it in two and linking 'the work of the ministry' with 'the equipment of the saints', is well supported by sound scholarship. In any case, 'ministry' here cannot refer to the preaching ministry, but means service in general (Gk. *diakonia*). The word translated 'to equip' literally means 'to fit together' or 'to bring something into its proper use' (Gk. *katartizein*). It is a word used outside New Testament literature by one Greek writer as a medical term meaning 'to set a dislocated joint'.

Not much imagination is needed to see the force of this analogy in relation to the life of the church. One has only to see how much harm can be done and hindrance caused to the work of God by one believer out of sorts spiritually, to realize how urgent is the need for a ministry in the church that can set such people right again. The same word is used several times in the New Testament also in deeply suggestive contexts. In the Hebrews Epistle[8] where it is said that the worlds were *created* (AV *framed*) by the Word of God, this is the word used, suggesting that as in the beginning the divine Word called worlds into being, so in the Word of the gospel God calls the new creation into being by His grace.

In the account of the call of James and John,[9] the disciples are said to have been busy *mending* their nets; again the word used is *katartizein*, and this also is a description of the work of the ministry — the mending of broken things, and making them serviceable again. Paul also uses the word when, in writing to the Galatians of the possibility of a believer being overtaken

[8] Heb. 11:3. [9] Mt. 4:21.

in a fault, he says: 'You who are spiritual should *restore* him in a spirit of gentleness.'[1] Christ has taken into consideration the eventuality of His children falling into sin, and has graciously instituted the ministry of the Word in His church to restore us to fellowship and usefulness. The lost coin in our Lord's parable[2] is brought back into circulation and enabled to fulfil its true function and the purpose for which it was minted.

Viewed in this light, the apostle's words define and elucidate the purpose of a true ministry of the Word as being to bring men and women into their real destiny in the purpose and intention of God, to fit them for His glad service and so build up the body of Christ that it will grow.[3] The profound, practical significance of this idea could scarcely be over-estimated. The growth of the body — this is true biblical evangelism, dynamic in its whole conception. A church shaped and fashioned by a ministry at depth is God's ordained instrument of evangelism in any age.

Maturity and fruitful service

Paul's theme, then, is spiritual maturity. In the phrase, 'attain . . . to mature manhood'[4] the word he uses has the force of 'reaching one's destination'. The 'mature man' is, according to the scholars, a corporate idea rather than individual and personal — although it is certainly as relevant for the individual believer — and, if so, the thought is of a fully-grown church going forth into service, terrible as an army with banners, and it reminds us that we serve best from spiritual adulthood in the work of the kingdom. Fruit-

[1] Gal. 6:1. [2] Lk. 15:8-10. [3] Eph. 4:16. [4] Eph. 4:13.

ful service flows from maturity of character. The evidences of immaturity mentioned here[5] — childishness, inconstancy, superficiality, lack of discernment — underline the need for growing up spiritually if any impact is ever to be made by the testimony of the church. This needs to be emphasized, for these things unfortunately remain as obstinate realities in many lives long after the more overt traces of worldliness and carnality have been set aside. It is precisely here, in the deeper reaches of human personality, that the faithful disciplines of the cross must do their work in re-creating the souls of men in the image of Christ. Childish Christians, those who are victims of spiritual tantrums, and who mistake what they call sensitive natures for a self that refuses to die, can never do great things for God; and those who are inconstant, tossed to and fro in periodic enthusiasms, superficial and undiscerning, persisting in living in the shallows instead of launching out into the deep, prove to be a liability, not an asset, to the gospel, and do more harm than good.

It is the ripe, mature believer who counts for God. Nor is this necessarily a question of age or length of experience, for some mature more in twelve months than others in as many years, because they submit their hearts to the probing discipline of the Word of God. Sometimes it takes dynamite to blast the childishness and inconstancy out of the system, but those who are prepared to endure the blasts (many, alas, are not) are really transformed into persons whose lives tell, wherever they are, and whatever they do.

This is the force of Paul's words when he speaks of the whole body being joined and knit together and

[5] Eph. 4:14.

making bodily growth.[6] This is the real evangelism as evidenced in the New Testament church, the impact of what men are, rather than what they do, upon the outside world. This very much needs to be learned in an age of streamlined techniques and top-heavy organization in evangelistic effort. Someone has said, 'The secret of effectual service is not overwork but overflow'; this overflow is the inevitable and spontaneous outreach of a life that, spiritually, has 'come of age'.

The attractiveness of the early Christians

Nowhere is this pattern seen more clearly than in the Acts of the Apostles, and nowhere is the outworking of the doctrine of the indwelling Christ more plainly manifested. Among the many impressive characteristics of the amazingly vital and dynamic life of the early church, three in particular may be instanced as crystallizing the practical outcome and implications of the classical doctrine of the believer's union with Christ in His death and resurrection.

The first of these is the manifest attractiveness that rested upon the lives of the early Christians. No-one can deny that the early church was on fire for God. Blazing purity was its only standard, and it scorched all hypocrisy, sham and unreality. But it was a fire that warmed as well as burned. There was something irresistibly attractive about it. The disciples had favour with all the people[7] and great grace was upon them all.[8] The grace of God shone in their lives, and men were drawn by it. They were lovable men. The Psalmist[9] prayed, 'Let the beauty (RSV 'favour')

[6] Eph. 4:16. [7] Acts 2:47. [8] Acts 4:33. [9] Ps. 90:17, AV.

of the Lord our God be upon us.' This was what characterized these first believers; the beauty of holiness was upon them. Holiness, rightly understood, is a beautiful thing, and its beauty is the beauty and tenderness of divine love. The saying 'All the world loves a lover' is just as true in the spiritual life as elsewhere. It is the loving heart that is attractive and lovable.

The hallmarks of sanctification

It is a matter of experience, however, that not all Christians are lovable and attractive. They may be upright, sincere and steadfast, and yet there is somehow a forbidding quality in their sanctification. Paul seems to admit the possibility of this distinction when he says: 'Why, one will hardly die for a righteous man — though perhaps for a good man one will dare even to die.'[1] The fruit of holiness may unquestionably be there, but it has a sour taste. There is a sanctification that is hard and metallic, and sometimes cold, harsh and strident, which is the very antithesis of New Testament experience and bears witness to the tragic perversion that is only too possible in the experience of the believer. It would be difficult to find words more suitable than the following to express the nature of this distinction:

> 'Deep tenderness of spirit is the very soul and marrow of the Christ-life. Without it, the most vigorous life of righteousness, and zeal, and good works, and rigid purity of morals, and missionary reform, and profuse liberality, and ascetic self-denial, and most blameless conduct, utterly fail to measure up

[1] Rom. 5:7.

to the Christ-life unveiled in the New Testament. . . . Without tenderness of spirit the most intensely righteous, religious life, is like the image of God, but without His beauty and attractiveness. It is possible to be very religious and persevering in all Christian duties, to be a brave defender and preacher of holiness, to be mathematically orthodox, and blameless in outward life, and very zealous in good works, and yet to be greatly lacking in tenderness of spirit. . . . Many religious people seem loaded with good fruits, but the fruit tastes green; it lacks flavour and October mellowness. There is a touch of vinegar in their sanctity. Their purity has an icy coldness to it. They seem to have a baptism on them but it is not composed of those sweet spices of cinnamon and calamus and cassia, which God told Moses to compound as a fragrant type of the real sweetness of the Holy Spirit. Their testimonies are straight and definite, but they lack the melting quality. Their prayers are intelligent, and strong and pointed, but they lack the heart-piercing pathos of the dying Jesus. The summer heat in them is lacking. They preach eloquently, and explain with utmost nicety what is actual and original sin, and what is pardon and purity, but they lack the burning flame, that interior furnace of throbbing love that sighs and weeps, and breaks down under the heat of all-consuming love. This all-pervading tenderness of spirit is not a novitiate grace. It is not a product of April but of October. . . .'[2]

[2] Quoted from *Tenderness of Spirit* (Oriental Missionary Society).

The drawing power of holiness

A good and fair test to apply in this connection is to ask oneself the question: 'Am I the kind of Christian that a man who had failed would instinctively shrink from and say, "Oh, no, I could not confide in *him*", or would he feel free to come to me in trouble?' It is said of our Lord that sinners gathered round Him, drawn, not repelled, by His holiness, and the presence of this freedom is the only guarantee that the holiness in a believer's life is really from God.

Barnabas, that good man and full of the Holy Spirit,[3] was thus named by the apostles because they recognized him to be 'the son of encouragement'.[4] The word used here in the Greek is one from which the word 'Counsellor' (AV 'Comforter'), as applied to the Holy Spirit, comes. Its meaning is 'Advocate', one who stands by us to help. Barnabas had the reputation of being the kind of man who could be relied upon to help in time of trouble. It was always a comfort and encouragement to have him near at hand. His holiness was radiant with the love of God, and there was a quite spontaneous sympathy in him that could communicate itself to those in need.

Undoubtedly this was the secret of the early church. It radiated love and therefore drew love and confidence from men. Love is, after all, a very practical thing, and the only real proof of its existence is that it should show itself to others. No man can be a loving person in theory or in principle. He is so, only in so far as he does deeds of kindness and mercy and compassion, and says words of encouragement to others. 'Love in loving finds employ.' As John puts it, 'If any one

[3] Acts 11:24. [4] Acts 4:36.

has the world's goods and sees his brother in need, yet closes his heart against him, how does God's love abide in him? Little children, let us not love in word or speech but in deed and in truth.'[5] This is the acid test and it is here that the problem arises. Most people see the force and relevance of this argument, but plead in self-defence: 'That is all very well, but I find it very difficult at times to show my feelings; it embarrasses me to do so.' This is very plausible, but it is a dishonest refuge in which to avoid the challenge of the Christian ethic. It embarrasses people to show their real feelings because to do so is to give away part of themselves, and this is what selfishness and self-centredness grudges most of all. It is in the common relationships of life that this is seen most clearly and felt most keenly. There are many Christians who have never learned to say 'Thank you' graciously, and who cause their best friends much distress by their apparent thoughtlessness and lack of gratitude, when they take so much costly love and friendship, and many other acts of love and consideration, for granted.

Self-absorption and hardness of heart

It is this unwillingness to give of oneself which causes the hardness of heart that is the opposite of the spirit of love. The real problem is a self that has not learned to die. So often we are too preoccupied with ourselves — our own interests, problems, distresses, tastes or pleasures — to have time to think of others, let alone love them. Anna Laetitia Waring's words penetrate to the heart of this searching challenge:

[5] 1 Jn. 3:17, 18.

'I ask Thee for a thoughtful love,
Through constant watching wise,
To meet the glad with joyful smiles,
And wipe the weeping eyes,
And a heart at leisure from itself,
To soothe and sympathise.'

'A heart at leisure from itself' — this means utter self-negation, and this is why it must again be insisted that such love is possible only on the other side of death. It was because the apostles had really died, and were raised up again to newness of life in Christ, that this glorious manifestation of grace and power rested upon all their experience. Only when this is present is there any real evidence that a death has taken place at all and that the message of the gospel has borne fruit in human hearts.

'Know thyself before God'

Another notable characteristic in the life of the early church was its reality. Something of the bedrock, down-to-earth quality which marked the apostles' experience may be gathered from the way in which Paul relates the believer's response of consecration to Christ to various practical aspects of Christian living. The note of reality is very plain. Speaking of the possibility of moral transformation by the renewing of the mind,[6] he says in effect that so often in the spiritual life it is our thinking about ourselves that is wrong. As one translation puts it: 'Don't cherish exaggerated ideas of yourself or your importance, but try to have a

[6] Rom. 12:2.

sane estimate of your capabilities by the light of the faith that God has given to you all.'[7]

The apostle is thinking of this particularly in relation to the disrupting influence such an attitude can have in a fellowship, and it may be recalled how the apostle John warned against Diotrephes, 'who likes to put himself first'.[8] But this is also one of the major problems of personal life, and there is nothing so calculated to cause trouble in one's own experience as persisting in holding unrealistic estimates of oneself, and refusing to face up to God-given limitations. Very often, of course, it is the relentless drive of an inferiority complex that expresses itself in high and exalted ideas of one's own importance, out of all proportion to reality. The problem of inferiority complex is more closely allied to self-centredness than most of us would like to believe, and although many factors of upbringing and environment may have combined to produce it, we must recognize the root of the problem for what it is.

This is why, ultimately, the gospel is the only true psychology, for no less a power can break the tyranny of self in the human heart. That is why Paul seeks to show that the grace of humility is a first-fruit of consecration. A true surrender to Christ shrinks our inflated ego to its proper size in relation to Him and to our fellows, and imparts reality to our lives. And it is always better to be real, even if 'being real' means being quite small, than to be an inflated, but unreal, creature. A 'real' person may be quite ordinary (how unwilling men are to be just that!), but at least he is solid reality, and cannot be made smaller than he is (even when people try to pull him down a peg or two); but a man with exaggerated ideas of his own

[7] Rom. 12:3, J. B. Phillips. [8] 3 Jn. 9.

importance is living in a dream world of unreality, from which he is liable to be rudely awakened at any moment. It needs only one pinprick to burst a balloon! There is often a great deal of unconscious dishonesty in Christian life, when men pretend to be something they are not, and this is one of the things that a true experience of the cross is meant to deal with in our experience. Sanctification, in this sense, is a movement towards reality in human life.

Progress towards true humanity

Above all, the life of the early church was characterized — and surely this is a paramount need in evangelical life today — by humanity. The deepest word that can be spoken about sanctification is that it is a progress towards true humanity. Salvation is, essentially considered, the restoration of humanity to men. This is why the slightly inhuman, not to say unnatural, streak in some forms and expressions of sanctification is so far removed from the true work of grace in the soul. The greatest saints of God have been characterized, not by haloes and an atmosphere of distant unapproachability, but by their humanity. They have been intensely human and lovable people with a twinkle in their eyes. One has only to read the biographies of men like Moody, or Spurgeon, or Hudson Taylor, to see how true this is.

Some people take themselves so seriously in the Christian life that they become unnatural and stilted, and the natural reaction that comes unbidden to the mind is: 'If only they would unbend a little!' The truest understanding of the biblical emphasis is to recognize that it is most of all saying: 'Be yourself.'

This needs to be remembered at a time when many believers, in their earnest concern for spiritual advancement, seem to have adopted the cult of imitating the piety of the seventeenth and eighteenth centuries. But God wants us to be contemporary, not historical, Christians, and the interests of the gospel are best served in us, not by imitating the saints of the past, but by assimilating all that was good in their testimony, and building it into our own lives, thus creating a contemporary and authentic Christian life, instead of one that is unnatural and unreal, veneered with a piety which, though the natural expression of a former age, cannot ring true today. We owe it to ourselves and to God to endeavour to reach a basic stratum of reality as a foundation for Christian character, for only thus can anything solid and true be built.

The fact that Christians sometimes seem to become progressively more stilted and unnatural shows how perilously easy it is to take a wrong turning in the life of sanctification, and how necessary it is to be aware of this danger and seek to obviate it. It cannot be too strongly emphasized that if spiritual considerations overlay our lives with unnaturalness, something terrible has happened, and we must at all costs break through it.

Reference has already been made[9] to the fact that the cross is a ' way out ' in the experience of the believer, and it is equally applicable in this connection. It is the way out of unnaturalness into a true humanity. In the absolute sense, it is true, there are no real men and women as yet; sin has robbed us of our humanity as well as of fellowship with God, and sanctification is simply the progress of its recovery. To be a believer means to be on the way, once more, to becoming human.

[9] See p. 65.

Recall to true manhood

The wonderful vision in Revelation of the new Jerusalem,[1] which speaks of the spaciousness and perfect proportions of the new order, may legitimately be interpreted as indicating, among other things, that the final consummation will mean a life in which all restrictions and cramping influences will be finally taken away from our experience, and true balance achieved. This is the ultimate hope and prospect for the Christian in glory, but glory is begun below, through grace, and we have the first-fruits of that newness by the Spirit. We should be showing forth at least something of this emancipation in our present experience. Salvation, however partial it may be in this life, should even now be setting us free from the crippling inhibitions of shyness and stilted behaviour which so often bedevil our relationships, and render true fellowship and natural friendships impossible. We owe it to ourselves and to our corporate testimony to attain this unaffected, basic humanity in our natural relationships with one another; and we are avoiding fundamental issues when we allow ourselves to think that this is not of supreme importance. We are called to be human in the best and fullest and truest sense, in all our attitudes and associations in the Christian life, and it is a tragic misunderstanding of the biblical doctrine of sanctification to think of it in any lesser terms. Nor can we ever be content until our union with Christ in His death and resurrection makes us so. Only in this way is it possible to magnify the Saviour.[2] As the telescope magnifies the distant star, so bringing it nearer to our gaze, so the believer has a responsibility to magnify Christ before men. It is

[1] Rev. 21:9ff. [2] Phil. 1:20, AV.

possible by the quality of transparent reality in our lives to bring Christ nearer to men, and make Him more real to them. This is the true evangelism, that builds up the church to His glory.

'No longer I, but Christ'

'The life I now live in the flesh I live by faith in the Son of God, who loved me and gave himself for me.'[3] The foregoing chapters have attempted to bring the teaching of the New Testament to bear on these words of the apostle. In the Introduction it was pointed out that there are two fundamental requirements necessary before growth and development are possible in the spiritual life — the exposition of the truth to the mind, and the moral submission of heart and will to that truth. This book will, to some extent at least, have accomplished the first of these requirements; and since the truth of God is both living and life-giving, never merely arid and intellectual, it is sent out in the faith and hope that the teaching it contains may lead to the other — the unreserved submission of the heart to the claims of Christ.

[3] Gal. 2:20.